THE GREAT
FOOTBALL
TRIVIA CHALLENGE

THE GREAT
FOOTBALL
TRIVIA CHALLENGE

600 QUESTIONS
TO TEST YOUR KNOWLEDGE

CHRISTOPHER PRICE

SPORTS
PUBLISHING

Sports Publishing books may be purchased in bulk at special discounts for sales promotion, corporate gifts, fund-raising, or educational purposes. Special editions can also be created to specifications. For details, contact the Special Sales Department, Sports Publishing, 307 West 36th Street, 11th Floor, New York, NY 10018 or sportspubbooks@skyhorsepublishing.com.

Sports Publishing® is a registered trademark of Skyhorse Publishing, Inc.®, a Delaware corporation.

Visit our website at www.sportspubbooks.com.

10 9 8 7 6 5 4 3 2 1

Library of Congress Cataloging-in-Publication Data is available on file.

Cover design by David Ter-Avanesyan
Cover photos credit: Getty Images

Print ISBN: 978-1-68358-499-5
Ebook ISBN: 978-1-68358-500-8

Printed in the United States of America

This one is for my friends—specifically, the ones who I get the honor of gathering with every March on Cape Cod. I'm blessed to have the greatest support system anyone could ever hope for. They're the kind of group that never says, "Why?" Instead, it's "What time do I need to be there?" or "How many books should I buy?"

Contents

Introduction

> Football fans share a universal language that cuts across many cultures and many personality types. A serious football fan is never alone. We are legion, and football is often the only thing we have in common.
>
> —Hunter S. Thompson

The first iteration of this trivia book (still in stores, and available online!) was published in 2019, and I'm proud to say it hit every major topic, from the history of the game and the lighter side of America's most popular sport to the NFL draft and Pro Football Hall of Fame. It was as all-encompassing as possible, with something for everyone. If it was half as much fun to read as it was to write, I know you guys must have had a ball.

But in the five years since, the game—and society—has changed. The world is more fragmented than ever. Whether it's with family, in the workplace, or with acquaintances, we're all just looking for something that can bind us together. From my viewpoint, more and more, it's clear the shared fandom that comes with football is one thing that can cement us these days, no matter the background. As Dr. Thompson wrote, it is a sport for everyone, a common ground. It's the connective tissue that cuts across the sporting landscape and can bring the unlikeliest of allies together.

If you're a Dallas fan, you can dismiss your old Texas uncle as out of touch, but every Sunday when the Cowboys play, you know he has your back. If I'm a Patriots fan, I can be walking through an airport in Atlanta and see someone else with a flying Elvis logo on their sweatshirt, and we can exchange a knowing smile and the understanding that the phrase "28–3" means a little more when you're passing through Southern Georgia. If I'm from western Pennsylvania and I'm in my first week at Ohio State watching the Browns play the Steelers, I know for sure the kid on the other side of the room wearing the Hines Ward jersey and I will have something to talk about.

It doesn't matter where you come from or what you look like, or how much money you make, or the kind of car you drive. As football fans, we are one. We speak a shared language: *Here we go, Steelers. San Diego ... Super Chargers! Bear down, Chicago Bears. Miami Dolphins, No. 1.* As a result, here's hoping this little book can help continue to bring football fans together in the best possible way.

As was the case with the first one, we tried to make this one accessible to all football fans. So regardless if you've been into the game since birth, or you started following a few years back, this book is for you. I hope everyone has fun trying to figure all these questions out.

Chapter 1

FOUR DOWNS—AFC

In the early 1970s, the AFC was seen as the lesser conference, the younger brother that the more esteemed NFC let be a part of the action via the NFL-AFL merger in 1970. But times have changed—teams like Miami, Oakland, and Pittsburgh altered the narrative in the 1970s and '80s. And now, we're in an era where eight of the last twelve Super Bowl champions have come from the AFC. The last two certified dynasties—New England and Kansas City—have come from the AFC. And while the AFC doesn't have a monopoly on the best young talent in the league, it's hard not to look at the list of the best quarterbacks under thirty—Mahomes, Burrow, Allen, Jackson, etc.—and not notice that they're all part of the same conference. This chapter takes a team-by-team look at the AFC, and some of the key people and situations that helped it grow.

AFC EAST

New England Patriots

1. Who was the first head coach in franchise history?
   A. Clive Rush
   B. Chuck Fairbanks
   C. Dick MacPherson
   D. Lou Saban
   Answer on page 17.

2. True or False: Bill Belichick never had a running back rush for 1,000 or more yards in back-to-back seasons in his 24 years as head coach of the Patriots.
   Answer on page 17.

3. Which NFL passing record does Tom Brady NOT hold?
   A. Oldest player to have thrown a pass in an NFL game.
   B. Most sacks taken in NFL history.
   C. Most career games won.
   D. Most Super Bowl wins.
   Answer on page 17.

4. Who was the first Black quarterback to start a game for the Patriots?
   A. Cam Newton
   B. Jacoby Brissett
   C. Onree Jackson
   D. Ron Burton
   Answer on page 17.

Buffalo Bills

1. True or False: The "run and shoot" was the name of the no-huddle offense the Bills ran under Marv Levy.
   Answer on page 17.

2. Which Bills player stripped Dallas' Leon Lett of the ball in embarrassing fashion near the end of Super Bowl XXVII?
   A. Don Beebe
   B. Steve Tasker
   C. Orlando Delicious
   D. Don Montgomery
   Answer on page 17.

3. Who was the Bills' first 1,000-yard rusher?
   A. Thurman Thomas
   B. O. J. Simpson
   C. Carlton "Cookie" Gilchrist
   D. Richie "Cake" Stevens
   Answer on page 17.

4. Which former Buffalo quarterback was the Republican Party's nominee for vice president in 1996?
   A. Jim Kelly
   B. Tyrod Taylor
   C. Jack Kemp
   D. Jack Frost
   Answer on page 17.

Miami Dolphins

1. In 2002, Ricky Williams set the Dolphins' single-season rushing record with 1,853 yards. Whose record did he break?
   A. Mercury Morris
   B. Jim Kiick
   C. Delvin Williams
   D. Johnny Gobbles
   Answer on page 18.

2. Who was the only 1,000-yard rusher Dan Marino ever had on his team?
   A. Karim Abdul-Jabbar
   B. Lamar Odom
   C. Lamar Jenkins
   D. Lamarr Hoyt
   Answer on page 18.

3. Which team lost 18 straight games in the Orange Bowl from 1966 through 1985?
   A. Buffalo Bills
   B. New York Jets
   C. New England Patriots
   D. Houston Oilers
   Answer on page 18.

4. True or False: Larry Csonka was the first player in franchise history elected to the Hall of Fame.
   Answer on page 18.

New York Jets

1. True or False: Fireman Ed is the name of the Jets superfan who has been leading the cheers at home games for years.
   Answer on page 18.

2. What was the name of the offensive lineman who Mark Sanchez knocked into, causing the infamous "Butt Fumble?"
   A. Brandon Moore
   B. Brandon Bass
   C. Sal Bass
   D. Brandon McGuirk
   Answer on page 18.

3. What was the nickname of the Jets' defensive line that was manned by Joe Klecko, Mark Gastineau, Abdul Salaam, and Marty Lyons in the early 1980s?
   A. Gang Green
   B. Shea Stadium Sack Attack
   C. New York Sack Exchange
   D. Hackey Sackers
   Answer on page 18.

4. Which Jets wide receiver was the first NFL player to reach 10,000 receiving yards?
   A. Al Toon
   B. Johnny "Lam" Jones
   C. Johnny Hector
   D. Don Maynard
   Answer on page 18.

AFC NORTH

Baltimore Ravens

1. True or False: The Ravens have a marching band.
   Answer on page 19.

2. Who was the Ravens' first-ever draft pick?
   A. Ray Lewis
   B. Tony Siragusa
   C. Justin Franklin
   D. Jonathan Ogden
   Answer on page 19.

3. Where did the Ravens play their home games after they relocated from Cleveland?
   A. Camden Yards
   B. Memorial Stadium
   C. M&T Bank Stadium
   D. Robert F. Kennedy Stadium
   Answer on page 19.

4. Who was the first head coach of the Ravens?
   A. Brian Billick
   B. Ted Marchibroda
   C. Rex Ryan
   D. John Harbaugh
   Answer on page 19.

Pittsburgh Steelers

1. Which Steeler was named MVP of Super Bowl X?
   A. Terry Bradshaw
   B. "Mean Joe" Greene
   C. Franco Harris
   D. Lynn Swann
   Answer on page 19.

2. Who was the first Steelers player voted into the Pro Football Hall of Fame?
   A. Johnny "Blood" McNally
   B. "Mean Joe" Greene
   C. Bobby Layne
   D. Mel Blount
   Answer on page 19.

3. True or False: Chuck Noll was the first coach in franchise history.
   Answer on page 19.

4. What is the name of the Steelers' mascot?
   A. Steeler Steve
   B. Steely McBeam
   C. Three River Pete
   D. Crusher
   Answer on page 19.

Cleveland Browns

1. What quarterback led the Browns to five straight playoff appearances in the 1980s?
   A. Brian Sipe
   B. Vinny Testaverde
   C. Todd Philcox
   D. Bernie Kosar
   Answer on page 19.

2. True or False: Bernie Kosar is the Browns' all-time leader in passing yards.
   Answer on page 20.

3. Which Browns backup quarterback was known as "Doctor Bomb?"
   A. Darren Levy
   B. Greg St. Martin
   C. David Mays
   D. Marvin Harrison
   Answer on page 20.

4. Who is the all-time sacks leader in Browns history?
   A. Swervin' Mervyn Fernandez
   B. Myles Garrett
   C. Clay Matthews
   D. Michael Dean Perry
   Answer on page 20.

Cincinnati Bengals

1. Who holds the franchise record for most catches in one season?
   A. Cris Collinsworth
   B. Chad "Ochocinco" Johnson
   C. Tee Higgins
   D. T. J. Houshmandzadeh
   Answer on page 20.

2. Which Bengal played six seasons with a steel rod in his leg after surgery?
   A. Rod Smith
   B. Steve "Old Steel Leg" Stevenson
   C. Hot Rod Williams
   D. Tim Krumrie
   Answer on page 20.

3. True or False: Carson Palmer holds the Bengals' franchise record for most career passing yards.
   Answer on page 20.

4. Which Cincinnati pass catcher out of Northeastern University had a pair of touchdown receptions for the Bengals in Super Bowl XVI?
   A. Cris Collinsworth
   B. Harvey Danger
   C. Dan Ross
   D. Gerry Brown
   Answer on page 20.

AFC SOUTH

Houston Texans

1. What year did the Texans join the NFL?
   A. 1996
   B. 1998
   C. 2000
   D. 2002
   Answer on page 20.

2. True or False: J. J. Watt and Andre Johnson had the same number of touchdown catches—three—in 2014.
   Answer on page 20.

3. Who is the franchise leader in rushing yards?
   A. Arian Foster
   B. Lamar Miller
   C. J. J. Watt
   D. Greg Levy
   Answer on page 20.

4. Who was the first Texan to be named NFL Defensive Rookie of the Year?
   A. J. J. Watt
   B. Mario Williams
   C. Brian Cushing
   D. DeMeco Ryans
   Answer on page 21.

Tennessee Titans

1. What was the name of the franchise before they became the Tennessee Titans?
A. Tennessee Tuxedos
B. Houston Oilers
C. Nashville Titans
D. Memphis Showboats
Answer on page 21.

2. In the 1996 NFL Draft, the franchise moved up to pick No. 14 to acquire running back Eddie George. What team did they make that deal with?
A. New England Patriots
B. St. Louis Rams
C. New York Jets
D. Seattle Seahawks
Answer on page 21.

3. Former Titans quarterback Steve McNair attended what college?
A. Northeastern University
B. Boston University
C. Alcorn State
D. University of Southern California
Answer on page 21.

4. What Titans receiver was tackled one-yard short of the goal line at the end of Super Bowl XXXIV?
A. Ian Lefferts
B. Charlie Joiner
C. Derrick Mason
D. Kevin Dyson
Answer on page 21.

Indianapolis Colts

1. Who was the first coach of the Colts after their move to Indianapolis?
A. Tony Dungy
B. Don Shula
C. Frank Kush
D. Dan Brem
Answer on page 21.

2. In 2002, Marvin Harrison broke the NFL's single-season record for receptions in one season. How many passes did he catch that year?
A. 110
B. 135
C. 143
D. 150
Answer on page 21.

3. Who scored the game-winning touchdown in the 1958 NFL Championship Game in overtime against the Giants?
A. Raymond Berry
B. Johnny Unitas
C. Art Donovan
D. Alan Ameche
Answer on page 21.

4. True or False: Mike Vanderjagt kicked the winning field goal to help lift the Colts to the win over the Cowboys in Super Bowl V.
Answer on page 21.

Jacksonville Jaguars

1. True or False: Jumpin' Jerry Jaguar is the official name of the Jacksonville team mascot.
   Answer on page 22.

2. Who is the Jaguars' all-time leader in rushing yards?
   A. Fred Taylor
   B. Maurice Jones-Drew
   C. Seth Schwartz
   D. James Stewart
   Answer on page 22.

3. What heavily favored team did the Jaguars upset in the 1996 playoffs to reach the AFC Championship Game against the Patriots?
   A. Buffalo Bills
   B. Pittsburgh Steelers
   C. Denver Broncos
   D. Indianapolis Colts
   Answer on page 22.

4. As of the end of the 2023 season, who has the most all-time wins as a head coach in Jaguars history?
   A. Doug Pederson
   B. Tom Coughlin
   C. Jack Del Rio
   D. Dom Capers
   Answer on page 22.

AFC WEST

Kansas City Chiefs

1. As of the end of the 2023 regular season, who held the franchise record for most receptions as a member of the Chiefs?
   A. Tony Gonzalez
   B. Travis Kelce
   C. Dwayne Bowe
   D. Otis Taylor
   Answer on page 22.

2. What Chiefs head coach played his college football at San Jose State?
   A. Dick Vermeil
   B. Hank Stram
   C. Marty Schottenheimer
   D. Todd Haley
   Answer on page 22.

3. True or False: As of the 2023 season, no one has more regular-season receiving yards in Chiefs' franchise history than Tyreek Hill.
   Answer on page 22.

4. How many playoff games did Joe Montana win as a member of the Chiefs?
   A. zero
   B. one
   C. two
   D. four
   Answer on page 22.

Las Vegas Raiders

1. This quarterback has thrown for the most yards in Raiders history
   A. Derek Carr
   B. Ken Stabler
   C. Daryle Lamonica
   D. Jim Plunkett
   Answer on page 22.

2. Which Raiders pass catcher carved out a niche as a favorite of Ken Stabler, and would later have the annual award for the top college receiver in America named in his honor?
   A. Fred Biletnikoff
   B. Paul "White Train" Howard
   C. Cliff Branch
   D. Dave Casper
   Answer on page 22.

3. Which Raiders linebacker slugged Patriots GM Patrick Sullivan after a 1985 playoff loss to New England?
   A. Jack Tatum
   B. Matt Millen
   C. Jason Lefferts
   D. Rocky Granato
   Answer on page 23.

4. Who was the Raiders' defensive player who was in on the tackle (and fumble) of Tom Brady near the end of the 2001 divisional playoff game that was later ruled an incomplete pass?
   A. Howie Long
   B. Warren Sapp

C. Charles Woodson
D. Darren Woodson
Answer on page 23.

Denver Broncos

1. What was the nickname given to the Denver defense in the 1970s?
   A. Orange Crush
   B. Rocky Mountain Way
   C. Homeland Defense
   D. Air Command
   Answer on page 23.

2. True or False: Dan Reeves won more than 100 games in the regular season as the Broncos head coach.
   Answer on page 23.

3. Who has the most regular-season sacks in Broncos history?
   A. Lyle Alzado
   B. Von Miller
   C. Karl Mecklenburg
   D. Elvis Dumervil
   Answer on page 23.

4. Who was the first member of the Broncos to rush for at least 20 touchdowns in a single season?
   A. Clinton Portis
   B. Bobby Hamilton
   C. Terrell Davis
   D. Mike Anderson
   Answer on page 23.

Los Angeles Chargers

1. Which head coach has led the Chargers to the most wins?
   A. Don Coryell
   B. Sid Gillman
   C. Marty Schottenheimer
   D. Paul Wonderman
   Answer on page 23.

2. Who was the first member of the Chargers inducted into the Pro Football Hall of Fame?
   A. Dan Fouts
   B. Sid Gillman
   C. John Jefferson
   D. Lance Alworth
   Answer on page 23.

3. True or False: The name of the Chargers' unofficial mascot for many years was nicknamed Mr. Reddy Kilowatt.
   Answer on page 24.

4. Which Chargers tight end has the most catches as a member of the franchise?
   A. Antonio Gates
   B. Kellen Winslow
   C. Hunter Henry
   D. Chuck Suede
   Answer on page 24.

Chapter 1

FOUR DOWNS—AFC

ANSWERS

AFC EAST

New England Patriots

1. D—Lou Saban.

2. True.

3. A—Oldest player to have thrown a pass in an NFL game. That record belongs to George Blanda.

4. B—Jacoby Brissett.

Buffalo Bills

1. False. It was called the "K-Gun."

2. A—Don Beebe.

3. C—Carlton "Cookie" Gilchrist.

4. C—Jack Kemp.

Miami Dolphins

1. C—Delvin Williams, who rushed for 1,258 yards for Miami in 1978.

2. A—Karim Abdul-Jabbar, who rushed for 1,116 yards in 1996.

3. C—New England Patriots.

4. False—As of 2024, there have been thirteen inductees to the National Football Hall of Fame that wore the Dolphins colors. The first was Paul Warfield, who was elected to the HOF in 1983. Four years later, Csonka and Jim Langer joined Warfield in Canton.

New York Jets

1. True.

2. A—Brandon Moore. The embarrassing event happened on Thanksgiving Night, on November 22, 2012 between the Jets and Patriots. Already down 20–0 in the second quarter, Sanchez ran directly into the derriere of Moore, fumbling the ball, which was recovered by Steve Gregory and taken to the house for a touchdown. The Pats would go on to embarrass the Jets on national television by a score of 49–19.

3. C—New York Sack Exchange. A dominant force, the Jets led the league in sacks in 1981 (66) and 1985 (49), with the former being the most by a team since the 1967 Oakland Raiders (67).

4. D—Don Maynard, who over 15 seasons—in both the AFL and NFL—collected 11,834 receiving yards.

AFC NORTH

Baltimore Ravens

1. True. They are only one of two franchises that has a marching band—the other being the Washington Commanders.

2. D—Jonathan Ogden was taken fourth overall by the Ravens in the 1996 NFL Draft. He would go on to play his entire 12-year career in Baltimore, and was elected to the Hall of Fame in 2013.

3. B—Memorial Stadium.

4. B—Ted Marchibroda coached the Ravens for their first three seasons in Baltimore (after coaching the Baltimore Colts from 1975–79), going 16–31–1.

Pittsburgh Steelers

1. D—Lynn Swann had four catches for 161 yards, leading the Steelers to a 21–17 victory in Super Bowl X over the Dallas Cowboys.

2. A—Johnny "Blood" McNally was the first Steeler elected into the Pro Football Hall of Fame, in 1963.

3. False. The Steelers had a dozen coaches between their inception in 1933 and when Chuck Noll took over in 1969.

4. B—Steely McBeam.

Cleveland Browns

1. D—Bernie Kosar led the Browns to the playoffs in five-straight seasons, from 1985 to 1989. They would go 3–5 in those games.

2. False. Brian Sipe is the team's all-time leader in passing yards, with 23,713. Kosar is third on that list, with 21,904.

3. C—David Mays, a practicing dentist, served as a backup to starter Brian Sipe.

4. B—Myles Garrett has 88.5 sacks through the 2023 NFL season. Second on the team's all-time list is Bill Glass, who collected 77.5 sacks from 1962–1968.

Cincinnati Bengals

1. D—T. J. Houshmandzadeh had 112 receptions for 1,143 yards in 2007. As of 2023, only two other players have had at least 100 receptions in a season (Carl Pickens in 1996 and Ja'Marr Chase in 2023—both with 100).

2. D—Tim Krumrie suffered a leg injury in Super Bowl XXIII and had a rod implanted after the game to stabilize the injury.

3. False. Ken Anderson has 32,838 passing yards. Palmer is fourth, with 22,694.

4. C—Dan Ross, who also set a then-record 11 catches in the Super Bowl against the 49ers.

AFC SOUTH

Houston Texans

1. D—2002.

2. True.

3. A—Arian Foster, with 6,472 rushing yards. He also had four seasons of 1,000-plus rushing yards in Houston.

4. D—DeMeco Ryans, who would eventually return to Houston once his playing days were over to become the team's head coach.

Tennessee Titans

1. B—Houston Oilers. After thirty-seven seasons in Houston—going back to the AFL—the franchise was moved to Tennessee. After two seasons as the "Tennessee Oilers," they would rebrand themselves as the Titans.

2. D—Seattle Seahawks. The Titans swapped first-round picks with Seattle (17 for 14) to move up and get George.

3. C—Alcorn State.

4. D—Kevin Dyson. With six seconds left and the Titans on the Rams' 10 yard line, Steve McNair hit a crossing Dyson for the catch. Just a few yards from glory, he reached the football in the hopes of breaking the end zone, but fell just a yard short, giving the Rams a 23–16 Super Bowl victory.

Indianapolis Colts

1. C—Frank Kush, who quit prior to the last game of the team's first year in Indy.

2. C—150. Harrison averaged roughly nine catches a game over the course of the 2002 season.

3. D—Alan Ameche. In what was dubbed "The Greatest Game Ever Played," Ameche scored to give the Colts a 23–17 win over the Giants at Yankee Stadium.

4. False. The 32-yarder was made by Jim O'Brien to help give the Colts their first Super Bowl victory.

Jacksonville Jaguars

1. False. The mascot for the Jaguars is Jaxson de Ville.

2. A—Fred Taylor had 11,271 rushing yards in his eleven seasons in Jacksonville, the most in franchise history.

3. C—Denver Broncos. Receiving a first-round bye, the 13–3 Broncos lost to the Jags in the divisional round, 30–27. Denver would go on to win Super Bowl XXXII the following season.

4. B and C—Both Tom Coughlin (1995–2002) and Jack Del-Rio (2003–11) collected 68 regular-season victories at the helm.

AFC WEST

Kansas City Chiefs

1. A—Tony Gonzalez had 916 career regular-season catches over his 12 seasons in Kansas City.

2. A—Dick Vermeil, who played quarterback for the school.

3. False. Tyreek Hill is fifth on the Chiefs' all-time list, with 6,630 regular-season receiving yards. Travis Kelce leads the way with 11,328.

4. C—2. Both of them came during the 1993 postseason, as he led Kansas City to victories over the Steelers and Oilers.

Las Vegas Raiders

1. A—Derek Carr. With 35,222 yards over nine seasons, Carr is atop the list of great Raiders quarterbacks. Second on the list is Ken Stabler, who is 16,144 yards behind Carr (19,078).

2. A—Fred Biletnikoff.

3. B—Matt Millen, while walking off the field after losing to the Patriots in the divisional round, saw a man get into the face of teammate Howie Long. Not knowing who it was, he pulled the man away from Long and slugged him in the face. Little did Millen know, it was then-Patriots GM Patrick Sullivan.

4. C—Charles Woodson. The future Hall of Famer stripped Brady for the fumble that *would* have won the game for the Raiders . . . had it not been overturned as the result of the "tuck rule."

Denver Broncos

1. A—Orange Crush. The combination of the orange jerseys and the popularity of the "Orange Crush" soft drink made for a natural nickname for the Denver defense. Sportswriter Woody Paige is credited with coming up with the moniker, which was give to a group that included the likes of Lyle Alzado and Randy Gradishar.

2. True: He finished with a regular-season mark of 110–73–1 as the head coach of the Broncos.

3. B—Von Miller has the team record for regular-season sacks, with 110.5.

4. C—Terrell Davis finished the 1998 season with 21 rushing touchdowns, which is still the fifth-highest total in NFL history.

Los Angeles Chargers

1. B—Sid Gillman, with 86 regular-season victories.

2. D—Lance Alworth was inducted into the Pro Football Hall of Fame in 1978.

3. False. He was played by Dan Jauregui, and nicknamed "Boltman."

4. A—Antonio Gates finished his career with 955 regular-season catches, the most in franchise history.

Chapter 2

FOUR DOWNS—NFC

The roots of the professional game sprung from the NFC; prior to the merger, it was the NFL, founded as the APFA in 1920 in Canton, Ohio. A circuit that began with dirt fields and leather helmets grew to survive and eventually thrive, fending off decades of competition to grow into the most powerful sports league in North America. It not only had the foresight needed to adapt, but the savvy leadership that knew when to fight off potential successors, and when to join forces. The 1970 merger between the AFL and NFL helped create the template for the modern-day NFL and help complete the move from a group that counted revenues in the thousands of dollars to one that is now a billion-dollar entity. This chapter helps chart the course of the NFC teams and reveals some of the most important people and places that helped shape the current NFL as we know it.

NFC EAST

New York Giants

1. Which quarterback has thrown for the most regular-season yards in Giants history?
   A. Phil Simms
   B. Eli Manning
   C. Joe Pisarcik
   D. Steven Kaye
   Answer on page 43–44.

2. True or False: Bill Parcells holds the franchise record for most wins with the Giants as a head coach.
Answer on page 43.

3. Lawrence Taylor was chosen second overall by the Giants in the 1981 NFL Draft. Who was taken first?
A. Ronnie Lott
B. Hugh Green
C. George Rogers
D. Mike Singletary
Answer on page 43.

4. Which former Giants receiver is credited with helping invent the "spike" touchdown celebration?
A. Stephen Baker, "The Touchdown Maker"
B. Phil McConkey
C. Homer Jones
D. Bhavan Suri
Answer on page 43–44.

Dallas Cowboys

1. True or False: The Cowboys play in the city of Dallas.
Answer on page 44.

2. Who has the most regular-season wins of any coach in franchise history?
A. Jimmy Johnson
B. Tom Landry
C. Mike McCarthy
D. Barry Switzer
Answer on page 44.

3. Emmitt Smith is the Cowboys' all-time rushing leader with 17,162 regular-season yards. Who is second in franchise history?
   A. Calvin Hill
   B. Ezekiel Elliott
   C. Tony Dorsett
   D. Herschel Walker
   Answer on page 44.

4. What Cowboys receiver did *not* wear the No. 88 in his time with Dallas?
   A. Michael Irvin
   B. Dez Bryant
   C. CeeDee Lamb
   D. Alvin Harper
   Answer on page 44.

Washington Commanders

1. True or False: The franchise has always considered Washington its home.
   Answer on page 44.

2. Which Washington quarterback did *not* win a Super Bowl when paired with Joe Gibbs?
   A. Doug Willams
   B. Gus Frerotte
   C. Mark Rypien
   D. Joe Theismann
   Answer on page 44.

3. Which Washington running back has the record for most rushing yards in a Super Bowl?
   A. Timmy Smith
   B. John Riggins
   C. Art Monk
   D. Antowain Smith
   Answer on page 44.

4. This former Washington defensive back and special teams star was considered the fastest man in football when he played in the 1980s and 1990s.
   A. Bob Hayes
   B. Darrell Green
   C. Deion Sanders
   D. Steve Jackson
   Answer on page 44.

Philadelphia Eagles

1. What year was the Eagles franchise founded?
   A. 1933
   B. 1935
   C. 1960
   D. 1972
   Answer on page 44.

2. True or False: Buddy Ryan was the first coach in franchise history to get the Eagles to the Super Bowl.
   Answer on page 44.

3. The "Body Bag Game" referred to a 1990 contest between the Eagles and what NFC East foe?
   A. New York Giants

B. Washington Redskins

C. Dallas Cowboys

D. New York Jets

Answer on page 45.

4. Who was the backup quarterback that ended up leading the Eagles past the Patriots in Super Bowl LII?

A. Carson Wentz

B. Jalen Hurts

C. Ty Detmer

D. Nick Foles

Answer on page 45.

NFC NORTH

Chicago Bears

1. Who is the Bears' all-time leader in regular-season passing yardage?

A. Jim McMahon

B. Jay Cutler

C. Jim Harbaugh

D. Sid Luckman

Answer on page 45.

2. Which running backs are currently ahead of Walter Payton on the all-time career rushing list?

A. Barry Sanders

B. Adrian Peterson

C. Emmitt Smith

D. Eric Dickerson

Answer on page 45.

3. What was the name of the song the Bears recorded in 1985?
   A. The Super Bowl Swing
   B. The Super Bowl Shuffle
   C. Bear With Us
   D. The Windy City Winners
   Answer on page 45.

4. True or False: Dick Butkus is the Bears' all-time franchise leader in sacks.
   Answer on page 45.

Green Bay Packers

1. In 1996, Brett Favre set an NFC record with 39 regular-season touchdown passes. Who was the previous record holder?
   A. Bart Starr
   B. Mark Rypien
   C. Brett Favre
   D. Randall Cunningham
   Answer on page 45.

2. Who did the Packers beat in Super Bowl I?
   A. Oakland Raiders
   B. Kansas City Chiefs
   C. Houston Oilers
   D. Miami Dolphins
   Answer on page 45.

3. True or False: Vince Lombardi was the founder of the Packers.
   Answer on page 46.

4. Who did the Packers beat in the Ice Bowl?
   A. Dallas Cowboys
   B. New York Giants
   C. Miami Dolphins
   D. Chicago Bears
   Answer on page 46.

Minnesota Vikings

1. Which one of these teams HASN'T beaten the Vikings in a Super Bowl?
   A. Oakland Raiders
   B. Kansas City Chiefs
   C. New England Patriots
   D. Miami Dolphins
   Answer on page 46.

2. True or False: Cris Carter had more career regular-season receiving yards in a Minnesota uniform than Randy Moss.
   Answer on page 46.

3. What was the nickname of the Vikings' defensive line in the 1960s and '70s?
   A. Purple Reign
   B. Purple People Eaters
   C. Grape Soda
   D. Minnesota Maulers
   Answer on page 46.

4. Who holds the franchise record for most regular-season interceptions in Vikings history?
   A. Paul Krause
   B. Harrison Smith
   C. Antoine Winfield
   D. Bobby Bryant
   Answer on page 46.

Detroit Lions

1. Barry Sanders is the all-time regular-season rushing leader in Lions history. Who's in second place?
   A. James Jones
   B. Billy Sims
   C. George Rodgers
   D. Dexter "The Hammer" Jenkins
   Answer on page 47.

2. What player supposedly put a fifty-year curse on the Lions?
   A. Andy Mahoney
   B. Greg Buttrey
   C. Bobby Layne
   D. Erik Hipple
   Answer on page 47.

3. What Lions receiver was nicknamed "Megatron?"
   A. Golden Tate
   B. Herman Moore
   C. Johnny Hector
   D. Calvin Johnson
   Answer on page 47.

4. True or False: Marvin Gaye once tried out for the Lions.
   Answer on page 47.

NFC SOUTH

Atlanta Falcons

1. True or False: "Falco" is the nickname of the Falcons mascot.
   Answer on page 47.

2. Who was the first head coach of the Falcons?
   A. Frederick Falconi
   B. Norb Hecker
   C. Barry Abercrombie
   D. Dan Reeves
   Answer on page 47.

3. Who is the all-time regular-season passing yardage leader
   in franchise history?
   A. Steve Bartkowski
   B. Michael Vick
   C. Matt Ryan
   D. Matt Schaub
   Answer on page 47.

4. Which coach has the most regular-season wins in the
   history of the Falcons?
   A. Mike Smith
   B. Arthur Smith
   C. Jerry Glanville
   D. Dan Quinn
   Answer on page 47.

New Orleans Saints

1. Who was the first player who played the majority of his career with the Saints to be voted into the Pro Football Hall of Fame?
   A. Joe Horn
   B. Drew Brees
   C. Walter Jones
   D. Rickey Jackson
   Answer on page 48.

2. Who is the Saints' all-time regular-season leader in passing yards?
   A. Drew Brees
   B. Archie Manning
   C. Aaron Brooks
   D. Derek Carr
   Answer on page 48.

3. Who is the franchise's scoring leader?
   A. Drew Brees
   B. Alvin Kamara
   C. Morten Andersen
   D. Will Lutz
   Answer on page 48.

4. True or False: The Saints have played their home games at the Superdome since their inception.
   Answer on page 48.

Carolina Panthers

1. As of the start of the 2024 season, the Panthers have retired one number in their franchise history. Who is it?
   A. Cam Newton
   B. Steve Smith Sr.
   C. Sam Mills
   D. Rickey Proehl
   Answer on page 48.

2. Who holds the franchise record for most passing yards in a season?
   A. Cam Newton
   B. Chris Weinke
   C. Steve Beuerlein
   D. Bryce Young
   Answer on page 48.

3. True or False: Tom Coughlin was the inaugural head coach of the Panthers.
   Answer on page 48–49.

4. What Hall of Famer did the Panthers successfully lure out of retirement in 2000?
   A. Reggie White
   B. Marcus Allen
   C. Jim O'Sullivan
   D. Steve Young
   Answer on page 49.

Tampa Bay Buccaneers

1. Who was the first player to be inducted into the Pro Football Hall of Fame as a Buccaneer?
   A. Lee Roy Selmon
   B. Steve Young
   C. Warren Sapp
   D. Doug Williams
   Answer on page 49.

2. What was the name of the legendary fullback who cleared the way for generations of Tampa Bay running backs— and still managed to pile up a ton of rushing yards (5,008) on his own?
   A. James Develin
   B. Mike Biglin
   C. Hank Watkins
   D. Mike Alstott
   Answer on page 49.

3. What two quarterbacks led the Bucs to wins in their two Super Bowl appearances?
   A. Tom Brady and Doug Williams
   B. Doug Williams and Brad Johnson
   C. Brad Johnson and Tom Brady
   D. Tom Brady and Kerry Collins
   Answer on page 49.

4. True or False: The original name of the character in the Tampa Bay Buccaneers logo was Captain Morgan.
   Answer on page 49.

NFC WEST

Los Angeles Rams

1. As of 2024, which one of these players *hasn't* had his jersey number retired by the Rams?
   A. Kurt Warner
   B. Eric Dickerson
   C. Jack Youngblood
   D. Jackie Slater
   Answer on page 49–50.

2. Who holds the franchise record for most career rushing yards in a Rams uniform?
   A. Eric Dickerson
   B. Steven Jackson
   C. Marshall Faulk
   D. Jon Tapper
   Answer on page 50.

3. What nickname *hasn't* been given to the Rams' fan base over the years?
   A. Ramily
   B. The Herd
   C. The Rammer Jammers
   D. Ram Nation
   Answer on page 50.

4. Rank these Rams head coaches in order of franchise wins, as of the end of the 2023 season.
   A. Jeff Fisher
   B. Mike Martz
   C. Dick Vermeil
   D. Sean McVay
   Answer on page 50.

Seattle Seahawks

1. How did the Seahawks get their nickname?
   A. They were named after their original owner, Joseph Seahawk.
   B. A public naming contest, which included submissions like Skippers and Lumberjacks.
   C. The original naming rights were sold to a local pet supply chain in the Northwest that came up with the name.
   D. The mayor threatened to have the funding for their proposed stadium pulled unless the team was named after his favorite animal.
   Answer on page 50.

2. Which receiver felt the wrath of Richard Sherman in a memorable postgame interview following the 2013 NFC title game?
   A. Michael Crabtree
   B. Torry Holt
   C. Mark Foster
   D. Anquan Boldin
   Answer on page 50.

3. What sport did former Seattle quarterback Russell Wilson think about playing before he went into football?
   A. Basketball
   B. Lacrosse
   C. Baseball
   D. Track & Field
   Answer on page 50–51.

4. True or false: The Seahawks played in the AFC briefly before moving to the NFC.
   Answer on page 51.

San Francisco 49ers

1. Who did Joe Montana beat out to become the starting quarterbacks for the Niners in 1981?
   A. Y. A. Tittle
   B. John Brodie
   C. Steve DeBerg
   D. Steve Bono
   Answer on page 51.

2. Where did the Niners play their home games from 1946 until 1970?
   A. Golden Gate Park
   B. Candlestick Park
   C. Levi's Stadium
   D. Kezar Stadium
   Answer on page 51.

3. Jerry Rice was the first Niner to score 1,000 points in his career with the franchise. Which kicker's scoring record did he break?
A. Tony Franklin
B. Ray Wersching
C. Matt Bahr
D. Garo Yapremian
Answer on page 51.

4. Which member of the 49ers' Super Bowl–winning team from the 1984 season was an elite track and field star who would have likely competed in the 1980 Olympics in the 110-meter hurdles if the US did not boycott the games?
A. Roger Craig
B. Renaldo Nehemiah
C. J. J. Stokes
D. Dwight Clark
Answer on page 51.

Arizona Cardinals

1. True or False: The Cardinals franchise started in Cleveland, moved to St. Louis, and then relocated to Arizona.
Answer on page 51.

2. Which Cardinal leads the franchise in receptions, receiving yards, and touchdowns?
A. Anquan Boldin
B. Larry Fitzgerald
C. Roy Green
D. Ernie Nevers
Answer on page 52.

3. Which quarterback led the Cardinals to their only Super Bowl appearance?
   A. Matt Leinart
   B. Jake Plummer
   C. Jim Hart
   D. Kurt Warner
   Answer on page 52.

4. Which franchise legend wore No. 40 for the Cardinals?
   A. Pat Tillman
   B. Aeneas Williams
   C. Kyler Murray
   D. Larry Fitzgerald
   Answer on page 52.

Chapter 2

FOUR DOWNS—NFC

ANSWERS

NFC EAST

New York Giants

1. B—Eli Manning threw for 57,023 yards over the course of his career with the Giants.

2. False. While Parcells had 127 regular-season wins for the G-Men, Steve Owen has the record with 153 in his 24 seasons at the helm.

3. C—George Rogers. Drafted by the New Orleans Saints, Rogers was a running back out of South Carolina. While he would win Rookie of the Year honors in 1981 after leading the league with 1,674 rushing yards, including two Pro Bowls and a ring with Washington in Super Bowl XXII, his career would pale in comparison to that of LT.

4. C—Homer Jones, who started firing the ball into the ground as part of his touchdown celebration routine starting in 1965. Jones would later say that he had to think of a new way to celebrate after the league passed a rule that a player would be fined

$500 for throwing the ball into the stands after celebrating a touchdown.

Dallas Cowboys

1. False. AT&T Stadium is in Arlington, which is approximately 20 miles from Dallas.

2. B—Tom Landry, who had 2,050 career regular-season victories with the Cowboys.

3. C—Tony Dorsett, with 12,036 career regular-season rushing yards.

4. D—Alvin Harper, who wore No. 80 in his first four seasons with Dallas (1991–94), then wore No. 82 in the two games he appeared with the team in 1999.

Washington Commanders

1. False. The team started as the Boston Braves in 1932 before moving to Washington, DC, in 1937.

2. B—Gus Frerotte. Gibbs is the only head coach in Super Bowl history to have won titles with three different quarterbacks.

3. A—Timmy Smith, who ran for 204 yards in Super Bowl XXII against the Broncos.

4. B—Darrell Green. The five-foot-nine defensive back (and Hall of Famer) was rumored to have run the 40 in 4.09 seconds.

Philadelphia Eagles

1. A—1933.

2. False. Dick Vermeil did it in 1980.

3. B—Washington. The nickname came from a pregame interview with Philadelphia coach Buddy Ryan who told reporters his team would inflict such pain on Washington that "they'll have to be carted off in body bags."

4. D—Nick Foles. After starting just five games in the 2018 season after an injury to starter Carson Wentz (in which he went 4–1), Foles led the Eagles to Super Bowl LII, winning it for the first time in franchise history.

NFC NORTH

Chicago Bears

1. B—Jay Cutler, with 23,443 passing yards.

2. C—Emmitt Smith. The Cowboys great is the only running back with more career rushing yards than Payton. Smith finished his career with 18,355 rushing yards, while Payton finished with 16,726.

3. B—The Super Bowl Shuffle.

4. False. Richard Dent tops the franchise list with 124.5 career sacks in the regular season. For the record, they didn't start officially counting sacks as a stat until the 1982 season.

Green Bay Packers

1. C—Favre broke his own record of 38, which he had set the year before.

2. B—Green Bay beat Kansas City, 35–10, in the first Super Bowl contest.

3. False—Earl "Curly" Lambeau is accorded as the founder of the franchise, as he was the one who initially solicited funds for team uniforms from his employer, the Indian Packing Company.

4. A—Bart Starr executed a perfect quarterback sneak—with some help from Jerry Kramer—to lift Green Bay past Dallas on December 31, 1967.

Minnesota Vikings

1. C—New England Patriots. The Vikings have made it to four Super Bowls in their otherwise illustrious history. They fell to the Chiefs in Super Bowl IV (23–7), the Dolphins in Super Bowl VIII (24–7), the Steelers in Super Bowl IX (16–6), and the Raiders in Super Bowl XI (32–14).

2. True. While Moss has more *career* receiving yards (15,292) than Carter (13,899), Carter has more (12,383) than Moss (9,316) in the purple and gold.

3. B—Purple People Eaters. From 1967 to 1977, the group dominated the NFL. In that eleven-season span, their defense ranked first in points allowed three times (1969–71), yards allowed three times (1969, 1970, 1975), and were top ten in points allowed nine times, yards allowed eight times, and touchdowns allowed per game nine times (with four Super Bowl appearances).

4. A—Paul Krause, who had 53 interceptions over his decade-plus in Minnesota (and holds the NFL record for most career interceptions, with 81). Second on the list is Krause's former teammate, Bobby Bryant, with 51.

Detroit Lions

1. B—Billy Sims racked up 5,106 rushing yards in Detroit—one more than Dexter Bussey. However, Sanders's 15,269 is more than the next three—Sims, Bussey, and Altie Taylor (4,297)—combined!

2. C—1958. The team traded Bobby Layne to the Steelers, and the quarterback reportedly said the Lions would "not win for fifty years." In the next half-century, Detroit finished with one of the worst winning percentages of any NFL team at .429.

3. D—Calvin Johnson. One of the most dominating wide receivers of his generation, Megatron averaged 86.1 yards per game during his career, which is the highest among players with at least 100 games played. And while only playing nine seasons in the league, was a unanimous Hall of Fame inductee in 2021.

4. True. The singer bulked up and tried to make the team in 1970, but ultimately failed to make the cut.

NFC SOUTH

Atlanta Falcons

1. False. The team's mascot is Freddie Falcon.

2. B—Norb Hecker. Leading the team in their first two seasons (1966–67), Hecker was fired after an 0–3 start to the '68 campaign, finishing with a 4–16–1 record (.133 winning percentage).

3. C—Matt Ryan threw for 59,735 passing yards during his career in Atlanta.

4. A—Mike Smith, with 66 wins. He also has the highest winning percentage for Falcons coaches at .589 (not including Wade Phillips, who coached the team for six games in 2003).

New Orleans Saints

1. D—Rickey Jackson played 13 of his 15 NFL seasons with the Saints, collecting six Pro Bowls. He was inducted into the Pro Football Hall of Fame in 2010

2. A—Drew Brees. Though spending the first five seasons of his career with the Chargers, Brees joined the Saints in 2006 and spent the next 15 years there, setting numerous records—including throwing for 68,010 yards.

3. C—Morten Andersen. Playing in the NFL for 25 seasons, up to the age of forty-seven, Andersen collected 2,544 points during his career—1,318 of those in NOLA.

4. False. Before playing at the Superdome in 1975, the team spent its first years playing home games at Tulane Stadium. Aside from relocations due to Hurricane Katrina and Ida, the team has called the Superdome home since the seventies.

Carolina Panthers

1. C—Sam Mills, whose No. 51 was retired by the team in 2005. He would be inducted to the Pro Football Hall of Fame four years later.

2. C—Steve Beuerlein, who joined the Panthers in 1996 (a year after they joined the league), threw for 4,436 yards in the 1999 season. The only other Panthers quarterback to throw for 4,000 yards is Cam Newton, who threw for 4,051 in 2011.

3. False. Tom Coughlin was the first head coach of the Jacksonville Jaguars, which entered the league the same year. Dom Capers was the first head coach in Carolina Panthers history (and was also the first head coach in Houston Texans history, when they joined the league in 2002).

4. A—Reggie White. Retiring after the 1998 season, White joined the Panthers in 2000, playing all 16 regular-season games and recording 5.5 sacks (bringing his career total to 198, which is second on the all-time list behind Bruce Smith with 200). He retired (again) after the 2000 season.

Tampa Bay Buccaneers

1. A—Lee Roy Selmon. The first overall pick in the 1976 draft by the Buccaneers for their inaugural season, Selmon played his entire nine-year career in Tampa Bay, being elected to the HOF in 1995. And while Sapp is known as a Buccaneers icon, both Young's and Williams's careers took off after they left the Bucs.

2. D—Mike Alstott. Nicknamed "A-Train," Alstott was a six-time Pro Bowler and three-time All-Pro fullback, spending his entire 11-year career in Tampa Bay. He was inducted into the Buccaneers Ring of Honor in 2015.

3. C—Brad Johnson and Tom Brady. While the latter is an obvious future Hall of Famer, Johnson leaned on his team's stellar defense to win Super Bowl XXXVII. In fact, of the fifty-two Super Bowl–winning quarterbacks who started at least 10 games, he ranks 34th in passing yards (3,047) and finished his career with a 72–53 record.

4. False. It was Bucco Bruce.

NFC WEST

Los Angeles Rams

1. A—Kurt Warner. Though leading the Rams to victory in Super Bowl XXXIV—the team's first championship since

1951—he has yet to have his number officially retired by the franchise.

2. B—Steven Jackson. Ahead of two Hall of Famers on the list—Eric Dickerson and Marshall Faulk—Jackson compiled 10,138 rushing yards during his nine seasons with the Rams, which included eight-straight 1,000-plus yard seasons.

3. C—The Rammer Jammers.

4. Sean McVay (70), Mike Martz (53), Jeff Fisher (31), Dick Vermeil (22)

Seattle Seahawks

1. B—A public naming contest, which included submissions like Skippers and Lumberjacks.

2. A—Michael Crabtree. After only playing in five regular-season games and being held to four receptions for 52 yards—including a pass to him being intercepted in the final seconds of the game by Malcolm Smith, off a tip by Sherman—Erin Andrews spoke to him after time expired about that game-winning play. "Well I'm the best corner in the game. When you try me with a sorry receiver like Crabtree, that's the result you gonna get. Don't you ever talk about me." When Andrews asked who was talking about him, Sherman continued. "Crabtree. Don't you open your mouth about the best, or I'm gonna shut it for you real quick!" The Seahawks would go on to win a decisive Super Bowl XLVIII over the Broncos two weeks later, 43–8.

3. C—Baseball. Drafted in the 41st round by the Baltimore Orioles in the 2007 MLB Draft—which included a $350,000 signing bonus—Wilson instead chose to attend NC State. He would again be drafted—this time in 2010 by the Colorado

Rockies—he would end up playing Class A ball in 2011, spring training with the Texas Rangers in 2014 and 2015, and with the New York Yankees in 2018.

4. True. Though a member of the NFC West in 1976—their inaugural season—they moved to the AFC West the following year, where they stayed until moving back to the NFC West in 2002.

San Francisco 49ers

1. C—Steve DeBerg. After two lackluster seasons as the team's starting quarterback in 1978 and '79 (for a combined 3–23 record), Montana started seven games in 1980 and became the team's full-time starter in 1981 (going 13–3).

2. D—Kezar Stadium, which was the first home of the 49ers before they moved into Candlestick Park in 1971.

3. B—Ray Werching, who scored 1,122 points in his career—979 of those with the Niners.

4. Renaldo Nehemiah, who won gold twice in 1979, at the Pan American Games and IAAF World Cup, for the 110 meter hurdles.

Arizona Cardinals

1. False. The franchise began as the Chicago Cardinals in 1920, first in the APFA and then the NFL. That was until 1960, when they moved to St. Louis (still as the Cardinals), and then to Arizona (as the Phoenix Cardinals from 1988–93, before going by Arizona).

2. B—Larry Fitzgerald. His 1,234 receptions, 15,545 receiving yards, and 110 touchdowns are all franchise records.

3. D—Kurt Warner. After three great years with the Rams—which included a victory in Super Bowl XXXIV—he had a 0–7 record in his last two seasons with the team. He then moved to the New York Giants in 2004, where he went 5–4 (before being benched for rookie Eli Manning). Joining the Cardinals the following season, where he went 8–18 over three seasons, he led the team to Super Bowl XLIII, where they fell to the Pittsburgh Steelers, 27–23.

4. A—Pat Tillman, who after four seasons in Arizona enlisted in the United States Army in the aftermath of the 9/11 attacks. Losing his life to friendly fire in 2004, he was awarded the Silver Start, Purple Heart, and Meritorious Service Medal for his service.

Chapter 3

DUETS

They say that if you want to go fast, go *alone*. If you want to go far, go *together*. With that in mind, it's important to note that some of the greatest successes in NFL history have occurred because of some classic partnerships. Tom Brady was great, but he was even better when Rob Gronkowski was added to the mix. Pat Summerall was a terrific broadcaster, but the duo of Summerall and John Madden was world class. And you can't tell the story of *Brian's Song* without Gale Sayers *and* Brian Piccolo. This chapter takes a look at some of football's best and most notable pairings, on and off the field.

1. Match these play-by-play men with their most well-known partners.

   1. Jim Nantz   A. Troy Aikman
   2. Pat Summerall   B. Cris Collinsworth
   3. Joe Buck   C. Bob Trumpy
   4. Mike Tirico   D. Merlin Olsen
   5. Don Criqui   E. John Madden
   6. Dick Enberg   F. Tony Romo
   Answer on page 67.

2. Match these famous celebrity football couples.
   1. Tom Brady   A. Hailee Steinfeld
   2. Travis Kelce   B. Simone Biles
   3. Joe Namath   C. Camille Kostek
   4. Russell Wilson   D. Ciara
   5. Josh Allen   E. Gisele Bundchen
   6. Jonathan Owens   F. Taylor Swift
   7. Christian McCaffrey G. Ann-Margret
   8. Rob Gronkowski   H. Olivia Culpo
   Answer on page 67.

3. Who were the only co-MVPS in Super Bowl history?
   A. Tom Brady and Adam Vinatieri
   B. Terry Bradshaw and Lynn Swann
   C. Joe Montana and Jerry Rice
   D. Harvey Martin and Randy White
   Answer on page 67.

4. The friendship between these two members of the Chicago Bears led to the inspiration for the movie *Brian's Song*.
   A. Walter Payton and Matt Suhey
   B. Maury Buford and Kevin Butler
   C. Gale Sayers and Brian Piccolo
   D. Buddy Ryan and Mike Ditka
   Answer on page 67.

5. There was no love lost between the Patriots and Ravens throughout the early stages of the twenty-first century, but no Baltimore defender seemed to love the fight more than:
   A. Terrell Suggs and Tom Brady

B. Ray Lewis and Antowain Smith
C. Ed Reed and Wes Welker
D. Haloti Ngata and Dan Koppen
Answer on page 67.

6. Offensive lineman Conrad Dobler had a beef with several players he went against in the late 1970s, but his chief antagonist was what Philadelphia defender?
   A. Herm Edwards
   B. Bill Bergey
   C. John Bunting
   D. Claude Humphrey
   Answer on page 67–68.

7. Jerry Rice's most productive seasons on San Francisco came when he was paired with which receiver on the opposite side of the field?
   A. J. J. Stokes
   B. Ricky Watters
   C. Deion Sanders
   D. John Taylor
   Answer on page 68.

8. In the mid-1990s, no rivalry between a defensive back and wide receiver was more fiercely contested than this one.
   A. Deion Sanders and Jerry Rice
   B. Rod Woodson and Michael Irvin
   C. Darrell Green and Tim Brown
   D. Steve Atwater and Mark Clayton
   Answer on page 68.

9. For three-plus seasons, which wide receiver/defensive back combination had some memorable battles as divisional foes in the AFC East?
   A. Keyshawn Johnson and Ty Law
   B. Wayne Chrebet and Vontae Davis
   C. Randy Moss and Darrelle Revis
   D. Wes Welker and Antonio Cromartie
   Answer on page 68.

10. Which legendary duo played together from 1956 to 1967 and combined for more than 600 pass completions?
    A. Otto Graham and Jim Brown
    B. Greg Levy and Darren Levy
    C. Y. A. Tittle and Armond Smith
    D. Johnny Unitas and Raymond Berry
    Answer on page 68.

11. What two quarterbacks are tied for second all-time when it comes to single-game passing yards in a regular-season contest?
    A. Matt Schaub and Warren Moon
    B. Tom Brady and Nick Foles
    C. Philip Rivers and Steve Young
    D. Jim McMahon and Joe Burrow
    Answer on page 68.

12. This legendary Pittsburgh play-by-play man served as the broadcast partner for Myron Cope for many years when it came to calling Steelers games. Who was he?
    A. Tim Benz
    B. Bill Hillgrove
    C. Mark Madden
    D. Joe Combellack
    Answer on page 68.

13. Bob Papa and Carl Banks have been calling the games on radio for this team since 2008.
A. New England Patriots
B. Cleveland Browns
C. New York Giants
D. Philadelphia Eagles
Answer on page 69.

14. Match the radio broadcast team (as of the end of the 2023 season) with the franchise

1. Brad Sham and Babe Laufenberg   A. San Francisco 49ers
2. Bob Socci and Scott Zolak   B. Dallas Cowboys
3. Bob Wischusen and Marty Lyons   C. Miami Dolphins
4. Greg Papa and Tim Ryan   D. Chicago Bears
5. Jimmy Cefalo and Joe Rose   E. Detroit Lions
6. Jeff Joniak and Tom Thayer   F. New York Jets
7. Dan Miller and Lomas Brown   G. New England Patriots

Answer on page 69.

15. Match the notable backup quarterback with the more famous starter(s):

1. Zeke Bratkowski   A. Tom Brady
2. Frank Reich   B. Bart Starr
3. Cody Carlson   C. Johnny Unitas and Bob Griese
4. Brian Hoyer   D. Jim Kelly
5. Earl Morrall   E. Warren Moon

Answer on page 69.

16. What NFC South duo paired for 240 passes, over 3,400 yards and 14 touchdowns in 2014 and 2015 combined?
    A. Drew Brees and Marques Colston
    B. Matt Ryan and Greg Olsen
    C. Cam Newton and Muhsin Muhammad
    D. Josh McCown and Mike Evans
    Answer on page 69.

17. What school produced two first-round picks at the same position in the 2007 NFL Draft?
    A. Alabama
    B. Southern California
    C. Tennessee
    D. LSU
    Answer on page 69.

18. The 2005 NFL Draft saw a pair of Auburn running backs taken in the top five. Who were they?
    Answer on page 69.

19. Which one of these school has NOT had at least one occasion where they've produced the top two picks in the NFL draft?
    A. Michigan State
    B. Nebraska
    C. Penn State
    D. Alabama
    Answer on page 69.

20. This receiver was one of Ben Roethlisberger's favorite targets in Pittsburgh; from 2013 through 2018 he had six straight seasons of 100 or more receptions, leading the league in catches twice.

A. Hines Ward
B. Antonio Brown
C. Heath Miller
D. JuJu Smith-Schuster
Answer on page 69.

21. In the Super Bowl era, who was the first rookie quarter-back/head coach duo to win their division?
A. C. J. Stroud and DeMeco Ryans
B. Tom Brady and Bill Belichick
C. Don Shula and Dan Marino
D. Bill Parcells and Phil Simms
Answer on page 69.

22. Patrick Mahomes and Travis Kelce and Tom Brady and Rob Gronkowski are two of the three QB/receiver (wide receiver or tight end) duos to start four-plus Super Bowls together. Who was the other pair?
A. Terry Bradshaw and Lynn Swann
B. Jim Kelly and Andre Reed
C. Roger Staubach and Drew Pearson
D. Peyton Manning and Marvin Harrison
Answer on page 69.

23. What family can boast of being the only father-son duo to win separate Super Bowl titles?
A. The Johnsons
B. The Kelces
C. The McCourtys
D. The DeOssies
Answer on page 70.

24. From 2007 through the early stages of the 2010 season, this duo powered the high-octane New England Patriots passing attack, but with a pair of wildly divergent styles.
   A. Wes Welker and Randy Moss
   B. Stanley Morgan and Darryl Stingley
   C. Brandon Tate and Josh Gordon
   D. Kendrick Bourne and DeVante Parker
   Answer on page 70.

25. In the early days of the twenty-first century, Dwight Freeney and Robert Mathis were a devastating pair of defensive ends for what team?
   A. Pittsburgh Steelers
   B. Green Bay Packers
   C. Indianapolis Colts
   D. New Orleans Saints
   Answer on page 70.

26. This duo set the NFL regular-season record for most receiving touchdowns.
   A. Terry Bradshaw and Lynn Swann
   B. Peyton Manning and Demaryius Thomas
   C. Pat Mahomes and Travis Kelce
   D. Tom Brady and Randy Moss
   Answer on page 70.

27. True or False: The Troy Aikman-to-Michael Irvin connection produced less than 50 *regular-season* touchdowns.
   Answer on page 70.

28. Who was Joe Namath's favorite target when he was with the Jets?
A. Emerson Boozer
B. John Boit
C. Don Maynard
D. Art Monk
Answer on page 70.

29. Lenny Moore and Alan Ameche were a dynamic duo that led what team to back-to-back NFL titles in 1958 and 1959?
A. New York Giants
B. Baltimore Colts
C. Detroit Lions
D. Los Angeles Rams
Answer on page 70–71.

30. What were the original names of Red Grange and Bronko Nagurski, who powered the Bears' legendary ground attack in the 1930s?
A. Harold Grange and Bronislau Nagurski
B. Gary Grange and Bruce Nagurski
C. Rodney Grange and Rodney Nagurski
D. Harvey Grange and Bobby Nagurski
Answer on page 71.

31. A pair of defensive linemen nicknamed "Danimal" and "Mongo" wreaked havoc together as part of the front seven of what team in the 1980s and 1990s?
A. Detroit Lions
B. Minnesota Vikings
C. Chicago Bears
D. Seattle Seahawks
Answer on page 71.

32. These two coaches—one a defensive coordinator and the other a head coach—reportedly came to blows during halftime of their team's only loss that season. Who were the coaches and what was the year?
    A. Chuck Noll and Tom Moore, 1979
    B. Mike Ditka and Buddy Ryan, 1985
    C. Mike Holmgren and Andy Reid, 1997
    D. Bill Belichick and Charlie Weis, 2001
    Answer on page 71.

33. What coach-quarterback tandem has produced the most Super Bowl wins?
    A. Chuck Noll and Terry Bradshaw
    B. Vince Lombardi and Bart Starr
    C. Bill Walsh and Joe Montana
    D. Bill Belichick and Tom Brady
    Answer on page 71.

34. Which coach-quarterback tandem never won a Super Bowl together?
    A. Don Shula and Dan Marino
    B. Fran Tarkenton and Bud Grant
    C. Marv Levy and Jim Kelly
    D. Dan Reeves and John Elway
    Answer on page 71.

35. What quarterback-receiver connection was the most prolific tandem when it came to touchdown receptions in regular-season NFL history?
    A. Peyton Manning and Marvin Harrison
    B. Tom Brady and Rob Gronkowski
    C. Patrick Mahomes and Travis Kelce

D. Dan Fouts and Kellen Winslow
Answer on page 71.

36. Who caught the most touchdown passes from Tom Brady in his career?
A. Julian Edelman
B. Rob Gronkowski
C. Randy Moss
D. Wes Welker
Answer on page 71.

37. This duo was consistently one of the most underrated receiving duos in the league, having played together on the West Coast from 1988 to 1993.
A. Andre Reed and James Lofton
B. Cliff Branch and Fred Biletnikoff
C. Isaac Bruce and Torry Holt
D. Flipper Anderson and Henry Ellard
Answer on page 71.

38. Match the quarterback with one of their favored pass catchers:
1. Joe Montana   A. Steve Largent
2. Jim Zorn   B. Charlie Joiner
3. Troy Aikman   C. Andre Reed
4. Dan Fouts   D. Jerry Rice
5. Jim Kelly   E. Michael Irvin
Answer on page 72.

39. What quarterback-pass-catcher duo currently has the mark when it comes to touchdown receptions in the postseason?
A. Joe Montana and Jerry Rice
B. Patrick Mahomes and Travis Kelce
C. Tom Brady and Rob Gronkowski
D. Terry Bradshaw and John Stallworth
Answer on page 72.

40. Who were the two Raiders running backs that formed a near-unstoppable tandem for four years in the late 1980s and early 1990s?
A. Marcus Allen and O. J. Simpson
B. Marcus Allen and Mark van Eeghen
C. Marcus Allen and Bo Jackson
D. Bo Jackson and John Higgins
Answer on page 72.

41. What pairing was known as the "Marks Brothers," one of the most devastating wide receiver duos of the 1980s?
A. Mark Duper and Mark Clayton
B. Mark Demoff and Mark Caritan
C. Mark Harris and Mark Wilson
D. Rodney Mark and Mark Wahlberg
Answer on page 72.

42. Regardless of the quarterback, these two Arizona receivers put up monster numbers in their six seasons together in the desert. Who were they?
A. Larry Fitzgerald and Anquan Boldin
B. Jackie Smith and Roy Green
C. Terrell Owens and Jerry Rice
D. Rob Moore and Larry Fitzgerald
Answer on page 72.

43. From 1987 through the 1992 season, when both Joe Montana and Steve Young were on the Niners roster, who started more regular-season games?
Answer on page 72.

44. These two receivers lit up the Metrodome together in the 1990s, but only one of them has his number retired by the Vikings. What are their names and which one has his jersey retired?
A. Cris Carter and Fred Smoot
B. Randy Moss and John Randle
C. John Randle and Cris Carter
D. Cris Carter and Randy Moss
Answer on page 72.

45. What Eagles pass-rush duo combined for 200 sacks between 1986 and 1992?
A. Jerome Brown and Seth Joyner
B. Clyde Simmons and Reggie White
C. Jeremiah Trotter and Andre Waters
D. Reggie White and Clyde Simmons
Answer on page 72.

46. What Rams receiving combination that was at the peak of their powers in the late 1940s and early 1950s included one player nicknamed "Crazy Legs."
A. Elroy Hirsch and Tom Fears
B. Elroy Face and Andre Jackson
C. Elroy Conti and Bill Dubinsky
D. Elroy Jetson and Cosmo Spacely
Answer on page 72.

47. A generation later, which pair of receivers for the Rams became a key part of the "Greatest Show on Turf?"
A. Isaac Bruce and Isaac Washington
B. Isaac Bruce and Torry Holt
C. Taylor Price and Ricky Washington
D. Terry Holt and Bruce Wayne
Answer on page 72.

48. This Raiders receiving duo helped light up the league in the 1970s.
A. Fred Toucher and Rob Poole
B. Lester Hayes and Jack Tatum
C. Jerry Rice and Tim Brown
D. Fred Biletnikoff and Cliff Branch
Answer on page 73.

Chapter 3

DUETS

ANSWERS

1. 1:F; 2:E; 3:A; 4:B; 5:C; 6:D

2. 1:E; 2:F; 3:G; 4:D; 5:A; 6:B; 7:H; 8:C

3. D—Harvey Martin and Randy White shared MVP honors after a Dallas win over Denver in Super Bowl XII, 27–10. Martin had a pair of sacks, while White added a sack of his own in the victory.

4. C—Gale Sayers and Brian Piccolo, who were portrayed in the movie by Billy Dee Williams and James Caan, were teammates on the Bears from 1966 to '69. The made-for-TV movie won four Emmy Awards.

5. A—Terrell Suggs and Tom Brady. Suggs called the Patriots' Super Bowl wins "questionable," needled him about the charges that alleged New England videotaped an opposing teams' practice, and took issue with the roughing the passer calls that Baltimore was flagged for when competing against Brady.

6. B—Bill Bergey. Bergey and Conrad Dobler had several notable tilts over the years; Dobler once kicked and spat on Bergey.

Bergey's career-ending knee injury came on a play where he was lined up opposite Dobler.

7. D—John Taylor. Taylor's nine-year career was impressive in its own right, but when paired with Rice—particularly from 1989 to 1991—they were two of the best pass catchers in the game. Taylor ended up with three Super Bowl rings and 347 catches in his career

8. A—Deion Sanders and Jerry Rice. The two stars engaged in some memorable matchups when Sanders was with the Cowboys and Falcons—and Rice was with the Niners. The two were also teammates in San Francisco for one season (1994).

9. C—Randy Moss and Darrelle Revis. Moss routinely steam-rolled the rest of the league, but from 2007 through 2010, Revis emerged as his counterpoint. Moss was one of few elite receivers who was routinely stranded on "Revis Island."

10. D—Johnny Unitas and Raymond Berry. Unitas and Berry helped lead the Colts to back-to-back championships in 1958 and 1959. Berry led the NFL in catches three straight seasons, from 1958 to 1960, while Unitas would be named All-Pro five times. The two men are enshrined in the Hall of Fame.

11. A—Matt Schaub and Warren Moon. Schaub tossed for 527 yards in a 2012 contest for the Texans against the Jaguars, while Moon threw for 527 yards in a 1990 game against the Chiefs.

12. B—Bill Hillgrove. Hillgrove and Myron Cope worked together calling Steelers games for many years. Hillgrove recently retired after 30 seasons in the booth. Meanwhile, Cope also gained a measure of fame for helping invent "The Terrible Towel."

13. C—New York Giants. The duo have been working together on Giants games as a two-man team in the booth since 2008.

14. 1:B; 2:G; 3:F; 4:A; 5:C; 6:D; 7:E

15. 1:B; 2:D; 3:E; 4:A; 5:C

16. B—Matt Ryan and Julio Jones. The duo were among the best in the game for three years, including in 2016—with Ryan walking away with an MVP, Jones was named to the Pro Bowl and an All-Pro, catching 83 passes for over 1,400 yards and six touchdowns.

17. D—LSU. It was a banner draft for the Tigers, as Dwayne Bowe was taken 23rd and went to Kansas City, and Craig Davis was chosen 27th overall by the San Diego Chargers.

18. Ronnie Brown was chosen second overall by the Miami Dolphins, and Cadillac Williams was taken at No. 5 by the Tampa Bay Buccaneers.

19. D—Alabama. The three other schools have all had one year where they've produced the top two picks in the draft. Michigan State had it in 1967, Nebraska in 1984, and Penn State in 2000. The Crimson Tide has yet to register that achievement.

20. B—Antonio Brown. Included in that stretch was a 2017 performance where he had one of the best seasons ever for a receiver, catching 136 passes for 1,834 yards and 10 touchdowns.

21. A—C. J. Stroud and DeMeco Ryans. The quarterback and coach turned the trick in 2023 with the Houston Texans.

22. B—Jim Kelly and Andre Reed. The quarterback and wide receiver started four together with the Bills in the 1990s, and were two of the most integral pieces of Buffalo's "K-Gun" offense that helped deliver four consecutive AFC titles.

23. D—Zak and Steve DeOssie. Both products of Boston College, Steve won it all with the Giants in Super Bowl XXV, while Zak took home the crown as part of a Giants team that won Super Bowl XLII.

24. A—Wes Welker and Randy Moss. The receivers combined to produce astronomical numbers in their three-plus years together with Tom Brady and Matt Cassel. Welker had a combined 432 regular-season catches from 2007 until the end of the 2010 regular season, while the 23 regular-season touchdown catches from Moss in 2007 is still an NFL record.

25. C—Indianapolis Colts. They were the NFL's most disruptive pass-rush pair from 2003 to '12. During that stretch, Freeney was tied for fourth in the NFL with 94.5 sacks and tied for third with 35 forced fumbles. Mathis was No. 6 with 91.5 sacks and tied for first with 38 forced fumbles.

26. D—Tom Brady and Randy Moss. In a record-setting 2007 season for the New England offense, the quarterback and wide receiver put on a show. Brady threw 50 regular-season touchdown passes, with a record 23 going to Moss.

27. True. Aikman hit Irvin with 49 career regular-season touchdown passes.

28. C—Don Maynard. The wide receiver caught 322 passes and 45 touchdowns in six seasons with Namath. The future Hall of Famer was at his best in the 1968 AFL Championship Game, when he caught six passes for 118 yards and two touchdowns to help the Jets past the Raiders and into Super Bowl III.

29. B—Baltimore Colts. The backfield duo of Moore and Ameche were vital to the Colts' successes in those remarkable years. Moore, a seven-time Pro Bowler, had a whopping 7.3

yards per carry in 1958. Meanwhile, Ameche rushed for a combined 15 touchdowns in those two seasons alone.

30. A—Harold Grange and Bronislau Nagurski were their given names.

31. C—Chicago Bears. Dan "Danimal" Hampton and Steve "Mongo" McMichael were an unstoppable duo for 10 seasons with the Bears, and helped shape a championship defense in 1985.

32. B—Mike Ditka and Buddy Ryan (1985). The two had a long-simmering feud that dated back several seasons, and apparently came to blows after a halftime argument during a 1985 game between Chicago and Miami. The contest ended up being the only loss of the season for the Bears.

33. D—Bill Belichick and Tom Brady. The duo won six Super Bowls together with the Patriots.

34. None. While all four had excellent careers, each combinations failed to win a Super Bowl.

35. A—Peyton Manning and Marvin Harrison. The two combined for 112 touchdowns in their 11 seasons together. Harrison had eight consecutive seasons of 10-plus touchdown catches in the regular season, a stretch that ran from 1999 until 2006.

36. B—Rob Gronkowski. The tight end, who was with Brady in New England as well as Tampa Bay, caught 90 touchdowns from Brady over the course of his career.

37. D—Flipper Anderson and Henry Ellard. The two helped bolster the Rams' passing attack over several seasons; Anderson still holds the NFL record for receiving yards in a game with 336 in 1989.

38. 1:D; 2:A; 3:E; 4:B; 5:C

39. B—Patrick Mahomes and Travis Kelce. As of the end of the 2023 season, Mahomes and Kelce have the lead with 16 touchdown connections in the postseason.

40. C—Marucs Allen and Bo Jackson. The duo were teammates with the Raiders from 1987 through 1990. Allen rushed for 12 touchdowns in 1990, while Jackson ended with 2,782 yards in just 38 games with the Raiders.

41. A—Mark Duper and Marck Clayton. The two formed the nucleus of the Miami passing attack in the 1980s. Clayton had 18 touchdown catches in 1984, and 14 in 1988, both tops in the league at the time.

42. A—Larry Fitzgerald and Anquan Boldin. In their six seasons together—from 2004 through 2009—they combined for 1,645 receptions, 13,210 yards, and 95 touchdowns.

43. Montana made 52 starts in those six seasons, while Young made 36.

44. D—Cris Carter and Randy Moss. Carter's No. 80 was retired by Minnesota, while Moss's hasn't been retired . . . yet.

45. D—Reggie White and Clyde Simmons. White had 21 sacks in 1987 and another 18 in 1988, while Simmons had 15.5 in 1989.

46. A—Elroy Hirsch and Tom Fears. Fears led the league in receptions from 1948 to 1950, while Hirsch had 1,495 receiving yards in 1951.

47. B—Isaac Bruce and Tory Holt. The receivers combined for 613 catches and 57 touchdowns in their first four seasons in the league.

48. D—Fred Biletnikoff and Cliff Branch. Biletnikoff had at least 750 yards receiving every year from 1967 until 1972, while Branch had 34 receiving touchdowns in the regular season from 1974 to 1976. Both are in the Hall of Fame.

Chapter 4

OUT OF BOUNDS

In life, like football, things don't always go according to plan. This chapter details the events that have gotten players, coaches, and others into hot water, both on and off the field.

1. True or False: Michael Crabtree and Aqib Talib came to blows during a 2017 game between the Raiders and Broncos because of Talib was trying to tear off a chain Crabtree was wearing around his neck.
    Answer on page 87.

2. What team was charged with the most penalties in a single game? For extra credit, how many and what year did it happen?
    A. New York Jets
    B. Oakland Raiders
    C. Seattle Seahawks
    D. Miami Dolphins
    Answer on page 87.

3. What Pittsburgh receiver blasted Cincinnati defender Keith Rivers with a blindside block in 2008 that left Rivers with a broken jaw?
    A. Antonio Brown
    B. JuJu Smith Schuster
    C. Hines Ward
    D. Santonio Holmes
    Answer on page 87.

4. What team has the record for most penalties in one 16-game season? For extra credit, name the amount of penalties and the year.
    A. The 2011 Oakland Raiders
    B. The 1996 Oakland Raiders
    C. The 1994 Los Angeles Raiders
    D. The 1998 Kansas City Chiefs
    Answer on page 87.

5. What team has the mark for the fewest number of penalties committed in a 16-game season?
    A. Dallas Cowboys
    B. New England Patriots
    C. Oakland Raiders
    D. San Francisco 49ers
    Answer on page 87.

6. The Bears engaged in a massive brawl with what team during a 1986 preseason game at Soldier Field?
    A. San Francisco 49ers
    B. New York Giants
    C. Washington Redskins
    D. St. Louis Cardinals
    Answer on page 88.

7. A deliberate spear from what Oakland defensive player on Kansas City quarterback Len Dawson sparked an all-out fight, and the nullification of a big Chiefs' gain?
   A. Ted Hendricks
   B. Jack Tatum
   C. John Matuszak
   D. Ben Davidson
   Answer on page 88.

8. True or False: The Raiders were one of the two teams involved in the October 1976 game that set the official NFL mark for most combined penalties in a game.
   Answer on page 88.

9. As of the end of the 2023 season, who is the most penalized player over the course of one season in NFL history, at least when it comes to on-field infractions?
   A. Jack Tatum
   B. John Matuszak
   C. Bob Golic
   D. Brandon Browner
   Answer on page 88.

10. Match the on-field combatants who have thrown down with each other over the years.
    1. Myles Garrett   A. Josh Norman
    2. Andre Johnson   B. Mason Rudolph
    3. Joey Porter   C. William Green
    4. Santana Moss   D. Corey Webster
    5. Odell Beckham Jr.   E. Cortland Finnegan
    Answer on page 88.

11. Name the two teams that played in "The Bounty Bowl" in 1989
    A. The New England Patriots and New York Jets
    B. The Dallas Cowboys and Philadelphia Eagles
    C. The Dallas Cowboys and Pittsburgh Steelers
    D. The Kansas City Chiefs and Oakland Raiders
    Answer on page 88.

12. Name the two teams that played in "The Body Bag Game" in 1990
    A. The New York Giants and San Francisco 49ers
    B. The New England Patriots and New York Jets
    C. The Philadelphia Eagles and Washington Redskins
    D. The Cleveland Browns and Pittsburgh Steelers
    Answer on page 88.

13. What Raiders linebacker slugged Patriots GM Patrick Sullivan after a game?
    A. Howie Long
    B. Jack Tatum
    C. Matt Millen
    D. Lyle Alzado
    Answer on page 89.

14. What Jets assistant coach was suspended after sticking his leg out and tripping a Miami player during a 2010 game?
    A. Sal Alosi
    B. Mike Pettine
    C. Bill Callahan
    D. Mike Westhoff
    Answer on page 89.

15. Which Dallas Cowboys wide receiver stabbed a team-mate with a pair of scissors because he allegedly had to wait in line for a haircut?
A. Alvin Harper
B. Michael Irvin
C. CeeDee Lamb
D. Drew Pearson
Answer on page 89.

16. Name the off-field issue or issues that have dogged the career of Miami Dolphins wide receiver Tyreek Hill.
A. Domestic assault
B. Paternity lawsuits
C. Alleged battery of a child
D. All of the above
Answer on page 89.

17. This running back was suspended for six games in 2014 for violating the league's personal conduct policy.
A. Leonard Fournette
B. LeGarrette Blount
C. Adrian Peterson
D. Le'Veon Bell
Answer on page 89.

18. What Dallas offensive lineman was once stopped by the police for having 213 pounds of marijuana in his van?
A. Larry Allen
B. Ron Stepnoski
C. Leon Lett
D. Nate Newton
Answer on page 89.

19. What charges has Albert Haynesworth faced away from the field?
A. Road rage.
B. Reckless boating.
C. Domestic assault.
D. All of the above.
Answer on page 89.

20. Green Bay legend Paul Hornung was suspended for one season for doing what?
A. Betting on league games.
B. Conspiring to throw games.
C. Assaulting a police officer.
D. All of the above.
Answer on page 89.

21. This player, who would later become a star of TV and movies, was among those who were banned for a season for gambling on pro football games.
A. Joe Namath
B. Alex Karras
C. Max McGee
D. Duke Castiglione
Answer on page 89.

22. What kicker was arrested in 2003 for misdemeanor assault, among other charges?
A. Adam Vinatieri
B. Sebastian Janikowski
C. Mike Vanderjagt
D. Jeff Ross
Answer on page 90.

23. What assistant coach was reportedly at the center of the "Bountygate" scandal that rocked the Saints during the 2009 season?
    A. Dennis Allen
    B. Sean Payton
    C. Gregg Williams
    D. Deuce McAllister
    Answer on page 90.

24. Offensive lineman Richie Incognito was suspended in 2013 for what incident?
    A. Bullying and harassment of teammate Jonathan Martin.
    B. Domestic assault.
    C. Punching an official.
    D. Violation of the league's substance abuse policy.
    Answer on page 90.

25. Former NFL linebacker Bill Romanowski was found culpable in which one of the following incidents?
    A. Punching a teammate in the eye during practice, forcing that teammate to eventually retire.
    B. Spitting in the face of an opponent during a game.
    C. Breaking the jaw of an opposing quarterback during a preseason game.
    D. All of the above.
    Answer on page 90.

26. Which one of Geno Smith's teammates punched the Jets quarterback during a locker room altercation in 2015?
A. I. K. Enemkpali
B. Damon Harrison
C. Antonio Cromartie
D. Sheldon Richardson
Answer on page 90.

27. Two players—Frank Filchock and Merle Hapes—were initially suspended from professional football for life after evidence found them guilty of associating with gamblers prior to the 1946 NFL Championship Game. What team did they play for?
A. Green Bay Packers
B. New York Giants
C. Philadelphia Eagles
D. Washington Redskins
Answer on page 90.

28. What Cincinnati player was suspended for the entire 1985 and 1987 seasons for violations of the league's drug policy?
A. Tim Krumrie
B. Eddie Brown
C. James Brooks
D. Stanley Wilson
Answer on page 90.

29. Who was hit with the longest suspension in league history for an on-field transgression?
A. Jack Tatum
B. Rodney Harrison

C. Vontaze Burfict
D. Adam "Pacman" Jones
Answer on page 90.

30. This Falcons receiver was suspended for the 2022 season for gambling on NFL games the previous year.
A. Julio Jones
B. Tim Mazzetti
C. Tim Dwight
D. Calvin Ridley
Answer on page 91.

31. What New York Giants receiver accidentally shot himself while in a nightclub in 2008?
A. Victor Cruz
B. Mario Manningham
C. Plaxico Burress
D. David Tyree
Answer on page 91.

32. What first-round pick in the 1982 NFL Draft went to jail after he retired because of a variety of charges, including forgery and theft?
A. Art Schlichter
B. Kenneth Sims
C. Chip Banks
D. Gerald Riggs
Answer on page 91.

33. Russell Erxleben was a punter and kicker taken in the first round of the 1979 NFL Draft. Why did he end up behind bars once his playing career was over?
A. Securities and investment fraud.
B. Beating up a mascot.
C. Public intoxication.
D. All of the above.
Answer on page 91.

34. What NFL coach was arrested during the 1985 season for "speeding, improper lane usage, and driving under the influence?"
A. Buddy Ryan
B. Mike Ditka
C. Sam Wyche
D. Bill Walsh
Answer on page 91.

35. This Raiders receiver initially faced a lawsuit after pushing a cameraman in the wake of a loss to the Chiefs at Arrowhead Stadium in 2022.
A. Henry Ruggs
B. Keelan Cole
C. Mack Hollins
D. Davante Adams
Answer on page 91.

36. In 2022, this quarterback was suspended six games for violating the league's personal conduct policy.
A. Tom Brady
B. Kirk Cousins
C. Deshaun Watson

D. Dak Prescott
Answer on page 91.

37. This linebacker was sentenced to one day in jail, three years of probation, and three hundred hours of community service for insider trading in 2018.
    A. Kyle Van Noy
    B. Jim Murray
    C. Patrick Queen
    D. Michael Kendricks
    Answer on page 91.

38. This former Steelers wide receiver was engaged in numerous off-field incidents that led to multiple suspensions over the course of his career.
    A. Antonio Brown
    B. Hines Ward
    C. Lynn Swann
    D. JuJu Smith-Schuster
    Answer on page 91.

39. In 1968, an entire officiating crew was suspended for a game and banned from working that postseason because of what gaffe?
    A. They didn't see someone come out of the stands and jump into a play.
    B. They lost track of downs.
    C. They started assaulting a player because of a misunderstanding.
    D. They flipped off a coach.
    Answer on page 91–92.

40. True or False: The league suspended an official one game for allegedly making profane and derogatory comments toward offensive lineman Trent Williams in a 2013 contest. *Answer on page 92.*

41. What New York Jets' player—albeit good-naturedly—once attacked the New England Patriots' mascot during a Pro Bowl event?
A. Antonio Cromartie
B. Bart Scott
C. Jamal Adams
D. Keyshawn Johnson
Answer on page 92.

Chapter 4

OUT OF BOUNDS

ANSWERS

1. True. Aqib Talib did it twice. Talib said years later the two eventually buried their beef when they happened to show up with their families at the same go-kart track. After some heated words, the two talked it out, and any lingering bad blood was apparently eliminated.

2. B—Oakland Raiders. In a 2016 game against the Tampa Bay Buccaneers, the Raiders were charged with 23 penalties, setting the mark.

3. C—Hines Ward. The wide receiver's hit left Rivers sidelined for the rest of the season, and added another chapter to the saga of the feud between the AFC North foes.

4. A—The 2011 Oakland Raiders. The team were flagged 163 times that season. The Raiders franchise has three of the top four seasons in this category.

5. B—The 2008 New England Patriots. Though not making the playoffs, even with an 11–5 record, the Pats took just 57 penalties that year to set the mark.

6. D—St. Louis Cardinals. A third-quarter skirmish between the two teams ended with one Chicago and three St. Louis players ejected, and fifty-one players fined.

7. D—Ben Davidson. Davidson's hit on Dawson led to a brawl and several ejections. After the fight, Oakland was able to rebound and kick a late field goal to tie the game. The hit eventually led to the creation of what was referred to as "The Davidson Rule," which prohibited defenders from "running or diving into, or throwing his body against or on a ball-carrier who falls or slips to the ground untouched and makes no attempt to advance, before or after the ball is dead."

8. False. That game, between the Buccaneers and Seahawks, produced a combined 39 penalties for 372 penalty yards.

9. D—Brandon Browner. The cornerback was flagged 24 times during the 2015 season as a member of the Saints, with 21 of the penalties accepted.

10. 1:B; 2:E; 3:C; 4:D; 5:A

11. B—The Dallas Cowboys and Philadelphia Eagles. Dallas met Philly in a game that had a wild buildup, which included Eagles coach Buddy Ryan placing a "bounty" on two Cowboys, Troy Aikman and Luis Zendejas. Philly won the game.

12. C—The Philadelphia Eagles and Washington Redskins. Philadelphia ended up capturing the victory in a contest where Eagles coach Buddy Ryan said his team was going to beat Washington so badly, "they'll have to be carted off in body bags." To that point, the Redskins suffered such a sound beating that they ended the game with running back Brian Mitchell at quarterback.

13. C—Matt Millen. Millen was frustrated after a playoff loss, and socked someone who he thought was taunting him after the game. Turns out, it was Sullivan.

14. A—Sal Alosi. During a December 2010 game between the Jets and Dolphins, Alosi stuck his leg out and tripped Miami gunner Nolan Carroll.

15. D—Michael Irvin. After coming in and finding teammate Everett McIver in the barber's chair, Irvin reported stabbed him when he wouldn't get up and allow Irvin to cut in line.

16. B—All of the above. According to multiple reports, Hill has been involved in all three situations.

17. C—Adrian Peterson. The running back was banned for six games after child abuse allegations, in which he admitted to using a switch to discipline his young son.

18. D—Nate Newton. Newton was pulled over by Louisiana police in November 2001 at a traffic stop, where it was discovered he had the marijuana with him in the car. A few months later, while out on bail, he was pulled over again with 175 pounds of marijuana in his car.

19. D—All of the above. The former defensive lineman has faced multiple charges stemming from off-field incidents.

20. A—Betting on league games. The halfback and future Hall of Famer was suspended for the 1963 season for betting on games. Hornung admitted to betting on horses, betting on college and NFL games, including on the Packers.

21. B—Alex Karras. He would go on to star on the TV show *Webster* and movie *Blazing Saddles*, would be hit with a season-long ban in 1963 for betting on league games.

22. B—Sebastian Janikowski. The kicker was arrested on suspicion of misdemeanor assault, misdemeanor vandalism, and public drunkenness after an altercation at a nightclub.

23. C—Gregg Williams. It was revealed in 2012 that Williams ran the bounty program that paid players who were responsible for injuries to opponents.

24. A—Bullying and harassment of a teammate. Incognito was banned for conduct detrimental to the team after it was found he was harassing teammate and fellow offensive lineman Jonathan Martin. He sat out the entire 2014 season.

25. D—All of the above. Romanowski was also sued by the IRS in 2023 for $15.3 million in unpaid back taxes.

26. A—I. K. Enemkpali. Enemkpali reportedly socked Smith because of a dispute over money. He was released by the team that day.

27. B—New York Giants. The day before the game, the two players—both with the Giants—were accused of taking bribes to fix the game. Both ended up playing most of the rest of their careers in the CFL.

28. D—Stanley Wilson. Wilson, who struggled with cocaine use over the course of his career, also missed Super Bowl XXIII because he was reportedly found in the throes of a cocaine high the night before the game. He was permanently banned by the league in May 1989.

29. C—Vontaze Burfict. After a helmet-to-helmet hit on Indianapolis' Jack Doyle in September 2019 when he was with Oakland, Burfict was suspended for the rest of the season, which ended up being 12 games.

30. D—Calvin Ridley. The young wide receiver was suspended for a season for betting on NFL games. He has since moved on to Jacksonville and Tennessee.

31. C—Plaxico Burress. The wide receiver was charged with attempted criminal possession of a weapon.

32. A—Art Schlichter. Taken fourth overall by the Colts, Schlichter was charged with committing over twenty felonies related to gambling.

33. A—Securities and investment fraud. Erxleben was convicted of securities fraud in 1999, and was again convicted of investment fraud in 2014.

34. B—Mike Ditka. The Hall of Fame coach was arrested in mid-October after flying home following a Bears win over the Niners.

35. D—Davante Adams. The charges were eventually dropped against Adams, and he was not punished by the league for the incident.

36. C—Deshaun Watson. Soon after signing with the Browns, Watson was banned for six games after he was accused of numerous cases of sexual misconduct.

37. D—Michael Kendricks. Kendricks pled guilty to one count of securities fraud and one count of conspiracy to commit securities fraud.

38. A—Antonio Brown. The much-maligned receiver was banned on several occasions, including for eight games in 2020 as a result of violations of the league's personal conduct policy.

39. B—They lost track of downs. This happened near the end of a Rams-Bears game and, as a result, Norm Schachter and his crew were suspended for a game and ruled ineligible for the playoffs.

40. True. Umpire Roy Ellison was sidelined for one game for allegedly calling Williams "garbage ass," among other things. Ellison was also involved in a 2018 incident involving defensive lineman Jerry Hughes.

41. C—Jamal Adams. The safety delivered the smackdown of "Pat Patriot" in early 2019.

Chapter 5

TWO-MINUTE DRILL

You know that feeling when you're jonesing for some hardcore NFL trivia, but don't have enough time to really get into minutiae? Then this chapter is for you. For the next series of questions, bring out the stopwatch and see how many of these rapid-fire queries you can get in two minutes or less; the winner gets a bucket of Gatorade dumped on their head and the honor of being trivia champ of our speed round.

1. How many divisions are there?
   Answer on page 109.

2. How long is regulation time for an NFL game?
   Answer on page 109.

3. How many games are played in an NFL regular season?
   Answer on page 109.

4. When did the league launch NFL.com?
   A. 1999
   B. 2000
   C. 2004
   D. 2009
   Answer on page 109.

5. What year did the NFL start using tablets along the sideline that provided high-resolution graphics to better prepare for an opponent?
A. 1999
B. 2007
C. 2009
D. 2014
Answer on page 109.

6. What NFL coach was presented with the first coach-to-quarterback electronic communication system in 1956?
A. Paul Brown
B. Vince Lombardi
C. Hank Stram
D. Dan Tanna
Answer on page 109.

7. What year did the league eventually approve the electronic communication system between coach and quarterback that was initially pioneered by Brown?
A. 1971
B. 1989
C. 1991
D. 1994
Answer on page 109.

8. What's the nickname given to the last pick in the NFL Draft?
A. Larry Lastpick
B. Lasty McPickeroo
C. Mr. Irrelevant
D. The Loser
Answer on page 109.

9. True or false: The league began the electronic communication system for the offense and defense simultaneously.
   Answer on page 110.

10. Who was the first broadcaster to use the telestrator?
    A. Cris Collinsworth
    B. John Madden
    C. Bob Trumpy
    D. Bill Parcells
    Answer on page 110.

11. What's the name of the football-themed site run by Mike Florio that has gained a massive following for up-to-date news and information?
    A. Pro Football Rumors
    B. Pro Football Talk
    C. Pigskin Chatter
    D. NFL News
    Answer on page 110.

12. What's the name of the parody Twitter/X account dreamt up by Barstool Sports meant to mock those who comment on Pro Football Talk?
    A. PFT Commenter
    B. Freddie Football
    C. Gronk69
    D. TD Tom
    Answer on page 110.

13. What data-driven site founded in 2004 by Neil Hornsby promised a new way to examine football statistics?
A. Gridiron Numbers
B. Pro Football Today
C. Inside the Numbers with Cris Collinsworth
D. Pro Football Focus
Answer on page 110.

14. This is perhaps the best-known stat from the website Football Outsiders, which analyzes data from across the world of professional football.
A. WAR (Wins over Replacement)
B. QBR (Quarterback Rating)
C. DVOA (Defense-adjusted Value Over Average)
D. TPS (Total Points Scored)
Answer on page 110.

15. True or False: Amazon acquired exclusive rights to broadcast *Thursday Night Football* in 2019?
Answer on page 110.

16. As of 2024, which NFL team has the most followers on X?
A. New England Patriots
B. Dallas Cowboys
C. Philadelphia Eagles
D. Pittsburgh Steelers
Answer on page 110.

17. What NFL Insider has the most followers on X?
A. Field Yates
B. Adam Schefter

C. Jason La Canfora

D. Jay Glazer

Answer on page 110.

18. In January 2017, which wide receiver created a furor when he live streamed a postgame scene in the locker room after a playoff win that featured his coach going on a NSFW rant against their upcoming opponent?

A. Chris Hogan, New England Patriots

B. Davante Adams, Green Bay Packers

C. Julio Jones, Atlanta Falcons

D. Antonio Brown, Pittsburgh Steelers

Answer on page 110.

19. What site served as the platform for the NFL's first regular-season streaming game in 2015?

A. NFL.com

B. ESPN

C. Yahoo!

D. Amazon

Answer on page 110.

20. Which streaming service was the platform for the NFL's first streaming-only playoff game?

A. Amazon

B. Hulu

C. Peacock

D. Netflix

Answer on page 110.

21. True or False: As of 2024, Travis Kelce has the most followers on Instagram of any active player.
Answer on page 111.

22. What three teams are not named for a city or state?
Answer on page 111.

23. What team has appeared in both the AFC and NFC Championship Games?
Answer on page 111.

24. What team has never had a quarterback throw for 4,000 or more yards or 30-plus touchdown passes in a season?
A. Seattle Seahawks
B. Chicago Bears
C. New York Giants
D. Los Angeles Rams
Answer on page 111.

25. What team is the worst in NFL history when it comes to point differential over the course of an entire season?
A. Tampa Bay Buccaneers, 1976
B. Baltimore Colts, 1981
C. New England Patriots, 1990
D. Cleveland Browns, 2000
Answer on page 111.

26. Which one of these running backs did NOT post a 1,000-yard season after the age of thirty?
A. Curtis Martin
B. Tiki Barber
C. Walter Payton

D. Shaun Alexander
Answer on page 111.

27. This wide receiver set the combine record for the fastest 40 time at 4.21. Who was he?
A. Jerry Rice
B. "Bullet" Bob Hayes
C. Xavier Worthy
D. Chris Johnson
Answer on page 111.

28. What do Brett Favre and C. J. Stroud have in common?
A. Their first career completions were to themselves.
B. They were both taken at the same spot in their respective drafts.
C. They both went to Southern Miss.
D. They both had Mike Holmgren as their rookie head coach.
Answer on page 111.

29. What left-handed quarterback has the most career passing yards?
A. Boomer Esiason
B. Jim Zorn
C. Steve Young
D. Ken Stabler
Answer on page 111.

30. What quarterback has the single-season record for the most interceptions?
A. Brett Favre
B. George Blanda
C. Tom Brady
D. Aaron Rodgers
Answer on page 112.

31. Who has the record for most touchdowns in a single season?
A. LaDainian Tomlinson
B. Shaun Alexander
C. Priest Holmes
D. Marshall Faulk
Answer on page 112.

32. True or False: Deion Sanders has the NFL record for most non-offensive touchdowns in a career.
Answer on page 112.

33. There are two players who are NOT in the Pro Football Hall of Fame who are in the top five all-time when it comes to all-purpose yards. Both are running backs—one of them played collegiately at Louisiana, and spent the bulk of his pro career with Washington, while the other spent most of his time in San Francisco after an impressive college career at Miami. Name them.
Answer on page 112.

34. What legendary receiver has more career tackles than dropped passes?
A. Jerry Rice
B. Randy Moss

C. Larry Fitzgerald
D. Terrell Owens
Answer on page 112.

35. This quarterback was originally drafted by the Patriots, who planned to turn him into a running back. He refused to move, and was traded. He later won an NFL MVP award. Who was it?
A. Brett Favre
B. Steve McNair
C. Steve Grogan
D. Rich Gannon
Answer on page 112.

36. What other college sport did Julius Peppers and Donovan McNabb excel in?
A. Basketball
B. Baseball
C. Golf
D. Volleyball
Answer on page 112.

37. Which quarterback threw four touchdowns in one game and intercepted the opposing quarterback four times in the same game?
A. Jim Thorpe
B. Sammy Baugh
C. Otto Graham
D. Gil Thorp
Answer on page 112.

38. Which quarterback holds the record for most passing yards in a single season (16 games)?
A. Tom Brady
B. Peyton Manning
C. Drew Brees
D. Ben Roethlisberger
Answer on page 112.

39. Which quarterback holds the record for most passing yards in a single season (17 games)?
A. Matthew Stafford
B. Patrick Mahomes
C. Justin Herbert
D. Tom Brady
Answer on page 112.

40. True or False: Among the official career sack totals compiled by the NFL, there's only one player—Jason Taylor—who is in the top ten for most sacks in a single season AND over the age of thirty.
Answer on page 113.

41. What quarterback under the age of thirty has thrown for the most yards in a single season, either 16 or 17 games?
A. Patrick Mahomes
B. Justin Herbert
C. Dan Marino
D. Jameis Winston
Answer on page 113.

42. What quarterback has the lowest QB rating in a winning effort in a Super Bowl?
A. Johnny Unitas

B. Brad Johnson
C. Ben Roethlisberger
D. Stan Humphries
Answer on page 113.

43. Five colleges have produced a Super Bowl-winning quarterback and a US president. Name them.
Answer on page 113.

44. Jerry Rice is one of three players in NFL history to catch a pass in their forties. The other two are not wide receivers—what position do they play?
Answer on page 113.

45. Jerry Rice is an easy choice when it comes to most receiving yards after the age of forty. But who is second all-time on that list?
A. Joey Galloway
B. Henry Ellard
C. George Blanda
D. Tom Brady
Answer on page 113.

46. Who has thrown for the most passing yards all time?
A. John Elway
B. Tom Brady
C. Drew Brees
D. Aaron Rodgers
Answer on page 113.

47. Who has the most receiving yards all time?
A. Terrell Owens
B. Randy Moss
C. Chad "Ochocinco" Johnson
D. Jerry Rice
Answer on page 113.

48. Who holds the single-season receiving yards record?
A. Randy Moss
B. Calvin Johnson
C. Darren Levy
D. Darren Sproles
Answer on page 113.

49. Who holds the single-season rushing yards record?
A. Walter Payton
B. Marshawn Lynch
C. Dan Tapper
D. Eric Dickerson
Answer on page 113.

50. What two franchises have existed since the NFL was founded in 1920?
Answer on page 113.

51. Which franchise won the most games in the 1970s?
A. Pittsburgh Steelers
B. Dallas Cowboys
C. Minnesota Vikings
D. Green Bay Packers
Answer on page 113.

52. Which franchise lost the most games in the 1970s?
A. Denver Broncos
B. New England Patriots
C. San Diego Chargers
D. New Orleans Saints
Answer on page 113.

53. Which franchise won the most games in the 1980s?
A. San Francisco 49ers
B. Seattle Seahawks
C. Minnesota Vikings
D. New York Giants
Answer on page 114.

54. Which franchise lost the most games in the 1980s?
A. Seattle Seahawks
B. Chicago Bears
C. Miami Dolphins
D. Tampa Bay Buccaneers
Answer on page 114.

55. Which franchise won the most games in the 1990s?
A. New York Jets
B. St. Louis Rams
C. San Francisco 49ers
D. Denver Broncos
Answer on page 114.

56. Which franchise lost the most games in the 1990s?
A. New Orleans Saints
B. New England Patriots
C. Cincinnati Bengals
D. Los Angeles/St. Louis Rams
Answer on page 114.

57. Which franchise won the most games in the 2000s?
A. Indianapolis Colts
B. New England Patriots
C. San Diego Chargers
D. Tennessee Titans
Answer on page 114.

58. Which franchise lost the most games in the 2000s?
A. Detroit Lions
B. Cleveland Browns
C. Kansas City Chiefs
D. Indianapolis Colts
Answer on page 114.

59. Which franchise won the most games in the 2010s?
A. Denver Broncos
B. New England Patriots
C. Seattle Seahawks
D. Tennessee Titans
Answer on page 114.

60. Which franchise lost the most games in the 2010s?
A. Philadelphia Eagles
B. Atlanta Falcons
C. Denver Broncos
D. Cleveland Browns
Answer on page 114.

61. Where is the Pro Football Hall of Fame?
A. Canton, Ohio
B. Hibbing, Minnesota
C. Dubuque, Iowa

D. Kansas City, Missouri
Answer on page 114.

62. How many different states have an NFL team?
    A. 18
    B. 23
    C. 27
    D. 29
    Answer on page 114.

63. Only two teams have purple as the predominant color in their uniform. Name them.
    Answer on page 114.

64. Who coined the term *sack*?
    A. Bruce Smith
    B. Mean Joe Greene
    C. Sammy "The Sackmaster" Tapper
    D. Deacon Jones
    Answer on page 114.

65. Four teams in the NFL are named after cats. What are they?
    Answer on page 114.

66. How many NFL stadiums are there in the United States?
    Answer on page 114.

67. True or False: Only one team plays its home games in New York.
    Answer on page 114.

68. Which state has the most NFL stadiums?
Answer on page 114.

69. How many stadiums are domes?
A. 6
B. 8
C. 10
D. 12
Answer on page 114.

70. How many of those domes have a retractable roof?
A. 2
B. 4
C. 5
D. 8
Answer on page 115.

71. What official was known for wearing tight shirts and flexing for the cameras when it came to making on-field calls?
A. Ed Hochuli
B. Shawn Hochuli
C. "Greasy" Brian Toland
D. Jerome Boger
Answer on page 115.

72. True or False: The name "The Duke" has been imprinted on every NFL football since 1941 as a tribute to John Wayne, who was a big football fan.
Answer on page 115.

Chapter 5

TWO-MINUTE DRILL

ANSWERS

1. Eight.

2. Sixty minutes.

3. 272 total games—17 for each team (as of 2024).

4. C. NFL.com went live in 2004.

5. D—2014. Now an integral piece of technology for all teams, it was the first year all teams had sideline access to league-provided Microsoft tablets.

6. A—Paul Brown. A pair of Ohio inventors presented it to Brown in 1956. He used it three games before the technology was banned leaguewide by commissioner Bert Bell.

7. D—1994.

8. C—Mr. Irrelevant. Celebrating Mr. Irrelevant has become a cottage industry, one that includes an entire week of festivities for the last pick in the draft. "We established Irrelevant Week to drive home an important message—that it's not a negative to be picked last in the NFL draft; rather, it's an honor to be drafted at all," said event coordinator and former NFL player Paul Salata.

9. False. The league allowed the system to also be used between a coach and a defensive player.

10. B. John Madden. The Hall of Fame coach and beloved broadcaster first utilized it during the CBS broadcast of Super Bowl XVI between the Niners and Bengals.

11. B—Pro Football Talk, which is the go-to site for many around the league.

12. A—PFT Commenter.

13. D—Pro Football Focus. PFF has become the standard-bearer for many when it comes to measuring success and failure for many players.

14. C—DVOA. Football Outsiders, discovered by Aaron Schatz, created several new statistical measures that helped revolutionize the data around the game.

15. False. It was March 2021.

16. A—New England Patriots. With around 4.68 million followers (as of April 2024), the Pats are the most followed team in the NFL. In second are the Dallas Cowboys, with around 4.41 million.

17. B—Adam Schefter. As of early 2024, ESPN's Schefter had around 11 million.

18. D—Antonio Brown. Brown, whose video captured Mike Tomlin calling the Patriots "assholes" prior to a playoff game against New England.

19. C—Yahoo!

20. C—Peacock. The NBC streaming site was the exclusive home for a Chiefs-Dolphins postseason matchup in January 2024.

21. False. Odell Beckham Jr. has 17.5 million followers.

22. The New England Patriots, Carolina Panthers, and Tampa Bay Buccaneers.

23. The Seahawks, who appeared in the 1983 AFC Championship Game, moved to the NFC in 2002 and appeared in that conference's game in 2013 (when they won Super Bowl XLVIII).

24. B—Chicago Bears. Through the 2023 season, the Bears are the only team for a quarterback to not hit either milestone in a single season.

25. A—Tampa Bay Buccaneers (1976). The Bucs' point differential was -287, making it all the more remarkable is the fact that Tampa Bay is the only team in the top five that played a 14-game season.

26. D—Shaun Alexander. The running back topped out at 1,880 rushing yards at the age of twenty-eight with the Seahawks. All of the other backs listed had at least one season of 1,000 yards or more on the ground after turning thirty years old.

27. C—Xavier Worthy. A wide receiver out of Texas, Worthy set the mark in 2024. He was a first-round pick of Kansas City, taken 28th overall.

28. A—Their first career completions were to themselves. On September 13, 1992, Favre's pass deflected off a defender's helmet and landed right back in his hands. Favre lost seven yards on the play. On September 10, 2023, Stroud's first career NFL pass attempt was batted down at the line of scrimmage. He caught the ball and ran forward for a one-yard gain.

29. C—Steve Young. The quarterback tossed for 33,124 career passing yards and 232 touchdowns to lead all southpaws.

30. B—George Blanda. The Hall of Famer tossed a whopping 42 interceptions as a member of the 1962 Houston Oilers. He's the only quarterback in AFL or NFL history to throw 30 or more interceptions in two seasons—he tossed 30 picks in 1965, again with the Oilers.

31. A—LaDainian Tomlinson. The former Chargers running back finished the 2006 season with a remarkable 31 touchdowns, to go along with 1,815 yards. He would win both MVP and Offensive Player of the League honors, as well as making the Pro Bowl and a first-team All-Pro.

32. False. Legendary Bears kick returner Devin Hester finished his career with 20. Sanders is second overall with 19.

33. Bran Mitchell is second all-time with 23,330 yards, while Frank Gore is fifth with 19,992 yards.

34. C—Larry Fitzgerald. He had 29 career drops and 37 career tackles.

35. D—Rich Gannon. The Delaware product would go on to win the NFL MVP in 2002 as a member of the Raiders.

36. A—Basketball. Both of them were on teams that ended up reaching the Final Four—Peppers at UNC, while McNabb walked on at Syracuse.

37. B—Sammy Baugh. The quarterback turned the trick for Washington on November 14, 1943, in a win against the Lions.

38. B—Peyton Manning. The Hall of Famer threw for 5,477 yards in 2013 with the Broncos—one yard more than Brees's 5,476 yards in 2011 with the Saints.

39. D—Tom Brady. A forty-forty-year-old Brady threw for 5,316 yards with the Buccaneers in 2021.

40. False. Among the top ten single-season sack totals of all time, all of the defenders are under the age of thirty.

41. A—Patrick Mahomes. At the age of twenty-six, Mahomes threw for 5,250 yards in a 17-game season with the Chiefs. Winston holds the mark for most passing yards by a quarterback under thirty in a 16-game season—he ended the 2019 season with the Buccaneers throwing for 5,109 yards.

42. C—Ben Roethlisberger. His anemic 22.6 QB rating in Super Bowl XL against the Seahawks takes the honors.

43. Delaware: Joe Biden and Joe Flacco; U.S. Naval Academy: Jimmy Carter and Roger Staubach; Stanford: Herbert Hoover, Jim Plunkett, and John Elway; Michigan: Gerald Ford and Tom Brady; Miami of Ohio: Benjamin Harrison and Ben Roethlisberger.

44. Quarterback. It's Tom Brady and Brett Favre. While in their forties, Brady had one catch for six yards, while Favre had one of his own for negative two yards.

45. D—Tom Brady. Rice had 2,509 receiving yards after the age of forty. Second is Brady's six.

46. B—Tom Brady, with 89,214.

47. D—Jerry Rice, with 22,895.

48. B—Calvin Johnson, who had 1,964 in 2012.

49. D—Eric Dickerson, who had 2,105 in 1984.

50. Cardinals and Bears.

51. B—Dallas Cowboys.

52. D—New Orleans Saints.

53. A—San Francisco 49ers.

54. D—Tampa Bay Buccaneers

55. C—San Francisco 49ers.

56. C—Cincinnati Bengals

57. A—Indianapolis Colts.

58. A—Detroit Lions.

59. B—New England Patriots

60. D—Cleveland Browns.

61. A—Canton, Ohio.

62. B—23.

63. The Baltimore Ravens and Minnesota Vikings.

64. D—Deacon Jones. Jones is credited coming up with the term for tackling the quarterback behind the line of scrimmage. "We needed a shorter term," Jones once told a reporter. "I gave it some thought and came up with the term *sack*. Like, you know, you sack a city—you devastate it."

65. The Carolina Panthers, Cincinnati Bengals, Detroit Lions, and Jacksonville Jaguars.

66. 30. The Jets and Giants share MetLife Stadium, while the Rams and Chargers share SoFi Stadium.

67. True: The Bills. The Jets and Giants technically play in northern New Jersey.

68. Florida—Tampa Bay, Miami, and Jacksonville.

69. C—10.

70. C—5.

71. B. Ed Hochuli, who served as an NFL official from 1990 until 2017.

72. False. "The Duke" is named after former Giants owner Wellington Mara, whose nickname was "Duke."

Chapter 6

BREAKING BARRIERS

You can't tell the story of the NFL without talking about individuals like Kenny Washington, Amy Trask, Tom Flores, and others. This chapter salutes those who have crashed the party over the years, opening doors for future generations and doing their best to achieve true equality in the world of professional football.

1. Who was the first female CEO of an NFL team?
   A. Georgia Frontiere
   B. Amy Trask
   C. Myra Kraft
   D. Martha Ford
   Answer on page 129.

2. What franchise—separately—had the first female CEO *and* team president?
   A. Kansas City Chiefs
   B. Denver Broncos
   C. Minnesota Vikings
   D. Las Vegas Raiders
   Answer on page 129.

3. Who was the first woman to serve as an on-field official in a Super Bowl?
   A. Sarah Thomas
   B. Lori Locust
   C. Gracie Hunt
   D. Dawn Aponte
   Answer on page 129.

4. Who was the first female sportscaster to be a part of an NFL pregame show?
   A. Robin Roberts
   B. Gail Roberts
   C. Phyllis George
   D. Andrea Kremer
   Answer on page 129.

5. Who was the first Black female sideline reporter on network television?
   A. Christina Pink
   B. Pam Oliver
   C. Jayne Kennedy
   D. Gayle King
   Answer on page 129.

6. Who was the first female to work as an analyst on an NFL broadcast?
   A. Melissa Stark
   B. Mina Kimes
   C. Jane Chastain
   D. Lesley Visser
   Answer on page 129.

7. Who was the first Black man to work as a sports analyst for an NFL pregame show?
   A. Greg Gumbel
   B. James Brown
   C. Beasley Reece
   D. Irv Cross
   Answer on page 129.

8. When did the NFL hire its first Black official?
   Answer on page 129.

9. These two women became the first all-female broadcast team to call an NFL regular-season game. Name the broadcasters and the year.
   A. Lesley Visser and Andrea Joyce, 1992
   B. Suzy Kolber and Erin Andrews, 1999
   C. Hannah Storm and Andrea Kremer, 2018
   D. Elle Duncan and Ashley Brewer, 2020
   Answer on page 130.

10. Who was the first female coach in the NFL?
    A. Jen Welter
    B. Sandy Cheeks
    C. Bryce Dickinson
    D. Kim Allen
    Answer on page 130.

11. True or False: A woman has never been on the coaching staff of a team that's taken part in the Super Bowl.
    Answer on page 130.

12. Match each head coach to the team where they served as the first Black coach in franchise history.

1. Jerod Mayo	A. Buccaneers
2. Art Shell	B. Bears
3. Dennis Green	C. Patriots
4. Tony Dungy	D. Eagles
5. Mike Tomlin	E. Bengals
6. Brian Flores	F. Lions
7. Jim Caldwell	G. Vikings
8. Marvin Lewis	H. Steelers
9. Ray Rhodes	I. Raiders
10. Lovie Smith	J. Dolphins

Answer on page 130.

13. What was the last NFL team to integrate?
   A. Washington Redskins
   B. New York Giants
   C. Dallas Cowboys
   D. Kansas City Chiefs
   Answer on page 130.

14. Who was the first Black player to be drafted into the NFL?
   A. Kenny Washington
   B. George Taliaferro
   C. Marion Motley
   D. Winston Jones
   Answer on page 130.

15. Who was the first player from an HBCU to be taken with the No. 1 pick in the NFL Draft?
   A. Alan Page

B. Richard Dent

C. Ed "Too Tall" Jones

D. Deion Sanders

Answer on page 130.

16. Who was the first athlete from an HBCU to play in the NFL?

A. Marion Motley

B. Fritz Pollard

C. Jackie Robinson

D. Paul Younger

Answer on page 130.

17. What distinction did Lowell Perry land as a member of the Steelers?

A. First Black assistant coach in team history.

B. First GM in team history.

C. First team physician, who served for 34 seasons.

D. Scout who discovered "Mean Joe" Greene and Mel Blount.

Answer on page 130.

18. Who was the first Black player in the NFL?

A. Art Shell

B. Fritz Pollard

C. Jackie Robinson

D. Doug Williams

Answer on page 131.

19. What distinction does Susan Tose Spencer hold when it comes to the history of women in the NFL?
A. She served as the first referee of the Pro Bowl.
B. She invented the practice squad.
C. She negotiated the contracts for Vince Lombardi when the coach was with the Green Bay Packers.
D. She served as the vice president and general counsel of the Philadelphia Eagles in the early 1980s.
Answer on page 131.

20. Who was the first Black lineman to win all-league honors?
A. "Mean Joe" Greene
B. Deacon Jones
C. Harvey Williams
D. Bill Willis
Answer on page 131.

21. Who was the first Black draft pick to play in the NFL?
A. Wally Triplett
B. Tony Dungy
C. Marion Motley
D. Fritz Pollard
Answer on page 131.

22. Who was the first Black coach to win a Super Bowl?
A. Art Shell
B. Mike Tomlin
C. Tony Dungy
D. Raheem Morris
Answer on page 131.

23. Who were the first two Black head coaches to face off in the Super Bowl?
    A. Lovie Smith vs. Raheem Morris
    B. Tony Dungy vs. Lovie Smith
    C. Art Shell vs. Tony Dungy
    D. Leslie Frazier vs. Romeo Crennel
    Answer on page 131.

24. Which Black coach turned the Tampa 2 defensive philosophy into one of the most effective schemes of the modern era?
    A. Tony Dungy
    B. Dennis Green
    C. Mike Tomlin
    D. Jerod Mayo
    Answer on page 131.

25. True or False: Dennis Green was the youngest coach in NFL history to lead his team to a Super Bowl when he accomplished the feat in 1998.
    Answer on page 131.

26. Who was the first Black quarterback to start in the NFL during the modern era?
    A. Doug Williams
    B. Marlin Briscoe
    C. Tony Banks
    D. Aaron Brooks
    Answer on page 131.

27. Who were the signal-callers when the first two Black quarterbacks faced off in the Super Bowl?
    A. Doug Williams vs. Warren Moon
    B. Michael Vick vs. Randall Cunningham
    C. Patrick Mahomes vs. Lamar Jackson
    D. Patrick Mahomes vs. Jalen Hurts
    Answer on page 132.

28. Who was the first Black player to win Super Bowl MVP?
    A. Doug Williams
    B. Lynn Swann
    C. Franco Harris
    D. John Stallworth
    Answer on page 132.

29. Mike Carey is famous for what honor?
    A. Being the first Black referee in a Super Bowl.
    B. Working as the scout who signed such notables as "Mean Joe" Greene, Terry Bradshaw, and Lynn Swann.
    C. The invention of several important pieces of equipment that the league later made mandatory, including the mouth guard.
    D. Being the NFL's first assistant commissioner to Paul Tagilaibue.
    Answer on page 132.

30. Who was the first Black man elected to the Pro Football Hall of Fame?
    A. Jim Brown
    B. Emlen Tunnell
    C. Fritz Pollard
    D. "Mean Joe" Greene
    Answer on page 132.

31. True or False: Ozzie Newsome was the NFL's first Black GM.
Answer on page 132.

32. Who was the first Black general manager to win a Super Bowl?
A. Ozzie Newsome
B. Art Shell
C. Jerry Reese
D. Doug Williams
Answer on page 132.

33. What team is credited as having broken the color barrier in the NFL?
A. Los Angeles Rams
B. Kansas City Chiefs
C. Houston Texans
D. Pittsburgh Steelers
Answer on page 132.

34. True or False: Tony Dungy was the NFL's first minority head coach to win a Super Bowl.
Answer on page 132.

35. Who was the first Mexican-born player inducted into the Pro Football Hall of Fame?
A. Tom Flores
B. Tom Fears
C. Luis Zendejas
D. Jim Plunkett
Answer on page 132.

36. What event precipitated the decision to integrate the Los Angeles Rams prior to the start of the 1946 season?
Answer on page 132.

37. Who was the owner who was responsible for holding the line at segregation in the NFL for several years?
A. Walter Wilson
B. Joseph Sullivan
C. Victor Bream
D. George Preston Marshall
Answer on page 133.

38. Kenny Washington, who was hailed as the man who broke the NFL's color barrier in 1946, was known for playing what two positions?
A. Quarterback and punter
B. Tight end and defensive end
C. Wide receiver and safety
D. Tailback and defensive back
Answer on page 133.

39. As of 2024, which of these teams has never had a Black head coach?
A. Buffalo Bills
B. Tennessee Titans
C. Jacksonville Jaguars
D. New York Giants
Answer on page 133.

40. True or False: The league's first all-Black on-field officiating and replay crew came in a game in 2023.
Answer on page 133.

41. True or False: No Black women have been inducted into the Pro Football Hall of Fame
Answer on page 133.

42. Who was the first Soviet-born player in the NFL?
A. Sebastian Janikowski
B. Rolf Benirschke
C. Igor Olshansky
D. Terrell Owens
Answer on page 133.

Chapter 6

BREAKING BARRIERS

ANSWERS

1. B—Amy Trask, who landed the honor with the Raiders.

2. D—Las Vegas Raiders. Amy Trask served as CEO, and Sandra Douglass Morgan was team president.

3. A—Sarah Thomas, at Super Bowl LV.

4. C—Phyllis George. A former Miss America, she was named a co-host of *The NFL Today* on CBS in 1975.

5. B—Pam Oliver. The journalist joined the "NFL on Fox" broadcast team in 1995, working as the No. 1 sideline reporter for the lead broadcast team of Pat Summerall and John Madden.

6. C—Jane Chastain. She worked on an NFL telecast for CBS in 1974, and was the first woman to do play-by-play for a major network.

7. D—Irv Cross. A former cornerback for the Eagles who reached the Pro Bowl twice, he worked as a part of *The NFL Today* crew on CBS beginning in 1975.

8. In 1965. Burt Toler was the first.

9. C—Hannah Storm and Andrea Kremer (2018). Storm and Kremer were the ones on the call for a game that was broadcast on Amazon Prime.

10. A—Jen Welter. In 2015, Welter, a former women's pro player and two-time Team USA Olympic medalist, was named an assistant coaching intern with the Cardinals.

11. False. In 2020, Katie Sowers became the first woman to coach in a Super Bowl. She was an offensive assistant for the San Francisco 49ers in their loss to the Kansas City Chiefs.

12. 1:C; 2:I; 3:G; 4:A; 5:H; 6:J; 7:F; 8:E; 9:D; 10:B

13. A—Washington Redskins. With pressure to integrate, as the only franchise yet to do so, they drafted Syracuse running back Ernie Davis with the first overall pick in the 1962 draft. As ownership way worried about the younger's potential salary demands, they traded his rights to the Browns in exchange for African Americans Bobby Mitchell and Leroy Jackson

14. B—George Taliaferro. Taliaferro was taken in the 13th round of the 1949 NFL Draft by the Bears. However, he chose to play for Los Angeles of the AAFC for one season before joining the NFL.

15. C—Ed "Too Tall" Jones. Jones went to Tennessee State, and was the first overall pick in the 1974 draft by the Cowboys. He would finish his career with a Super Bowl ring, multiple Pro Bowl berths, and 106 regular-season sacks.

16. D—Paul Younger. Nicknamed "Tank," Younger attended Grambling before joining the Rams in 1949. In his 10-year career in the NFL, he rushed for 3,640 yards.

17. A—First Black assistant coach in team history. Perry, who played one season for the Steelers, also worked as a scout for the franchise, and spent time as a TV analyst.

18. B—Fritz Pollard. The 5-foot-9, 165-pound back, who led Brown to the Rose Bowl in 1915, played and coached for multiple NFL teams. He was also the first Black head coach, in 1921, for the Akron Pros.

19. D—She served as the vice president and general counsel of the Philadelphia Eagles in the early 1980s. She also reportedly ran much of the day-to-day operations for the franchise.

20. D—Bill Willis. Playing for Cleveland at the time, he landed the honor in 1946. Willis would go on to win all-league honors seven times over the course of his career.

21. A—Wally Triplett. He was taken in the 19th round of the 1949 NFL Draft by the Detroit Lions. He played for the Lions and the Chicago Cardinals.

22. C—Tony Dungy. The Hall of Fame coach led the Colts to a win over the Bears in Super Bowl XLI.

23. B—Tony Dungy and Lovie Smith. The two squared off in Super Bowl XLI, where Dungy's Colts defeated Smith's Bears, 29–17.

24. A—Tony Dungy.

25. False. It was Mike Tomlin, who was six weeks shy of his thirty-seventh birthday when Pittsburgh defeated Arizona in Super Bowl XLIII. That record was eventually broken by Sean McVay of the Los Angeles Rams, who was just a few days past his thirty-sixth birthday when his team won Super Bowl LIII.

26. B—Marlin Briscoe, who did it with the Broncos in 1968. In his nine-year career, Briscoe played for the Buffalo Bills, Miami Dolphins, Denver Broncos, Detroit Lions, New England Patriots, and San Diego Chargers.

27. D—Patrick Mahomes and Jalen Hurts. The two met in Super Bowl LVII, where Mahomes's Chiefs defeated Hurts's Eagles, 38–35.

28. C—Franco Harris, who won it in 1975. Rushing for 158 yards and a touchdown on 34 carries, he helped his Steelers defeat the Vikings in Super Bowl IX, 16–6. He was also the first Italian-American to be named Super Bowl MVP.

29. A—Being the first Black referee in a Super Bowl. One of the most respected officials in the game, served as the first Black referee in a Super Bowl, landing the honor for Super Bowl XLII.

30. B—Emlen Tunnell. He was the first Black player in the history of the New York Giants. He was also the first Black player elected to the Pro Football Hall of Fame, landing the honor in 1967.

31. True. Ozzie Newsome was named GM of the Ravens in 2002.

32. C—Jerry Reese. He was the Giants' GM when they won Super Bowl XLVI.

33. A—Los Angeles Rams.

34. False. Tom Flores won two with the Raiders.

35. B—Tom Fears. He played for nine seasons—all with the Rams—and eventually became the first Mexican-born coach to become a head coach in the NFL.

36. Black newspapermen made the Los Angeles Coliseum Commission aware of the fact that the Rams did not have any Black players, and that the stadium, was supported by public funds. As a result, the stadium had to abide by an 1896 Supreme Court ruling, one that meant the stadium could not be leased to a segregated team.

37. D—George Preston Marshall. The then-owner of the Washington franchise, Marshall was vociferous in his decision not to integrate until he was forced. "We'll start signing Negroes when the Harlem Globetrotters start signing whites," he once said. Washington eventually agreed to integrate in 1962.

38. D—Tailback and defensive back. Washington played those positions for the Los Angeles Rams from 1946 to 1948.

39. All of them!

40. True. It happened in a Raiders-Chargers game in Las Vegas, on October 1, 2023.

41. True.

42. C—Igor Olshansky. A defensive end who entered the league in 2004, Olshansky played for the Chargers, Cowboys, and Dolphins. He finished with 12.5 sacks in his career.

Chapter 7

SUPER TRIVIA

The Super Bowl is the biggest North American sporting event of the year, becoming so much more than just a game. It's a cultural happening, the sort of annual event that crosses lines to include the hardcore football fan and the casual follower alike. Whether it's on the field, through commercials, the halftime show, or the memorable finish, it inevitably delivers some of the year's biggest sports memories. Check out this chapter to find out how well do you know your history of the big game.

1. Match the player with the game where he won Super Bowl MVP

   1. Terrell Davis
   2. Dexter Jackson
   3. Malcolm Smith
   4. John Elway
   5. Cooper Kupp
   6. Ottis Anderson
   7. Richard Dent
   8. Larry Csonka
   9. Deion Branch
   10. Santonio Holmes

   A. Super Bowl XXXIX
   B. Super Bowl XXXIII
   C. Super Bowl LVI
   D. Super Bowl XXXVII
   E. Super Bowl XX
   F. Super Bowl XXXII
   G. Super Bowl VIII
   H. Super Bowl XLIII
   I. Super Bowl XXV
   J. Super Bowl XLVIII

   Answer on page 153.

2. Match the performer (or performers) with the game where they headlined as the halftime artist.

1.	Diana Ross	A.	Super Bowl XLIX
2.	Bruce Springsteen	B.	Super Bowl XLVI
3.	U2	C.	Super Bowl XXXIX
4.	Prince	D.	Super Bowl XLI
5.	Madonna	E.	Super Bowl LVIII
6.	Katy Perry	F.	Super Bowl XXX
7.	Paul McCartney	G.	Super Bowl XXVII
8.	Usher	H.	Super Bowl XXXVI
9.	Michael Jackson	I.	Super Bowl LVII
10.	Rihanna	J.	Super Bowl XLIII

Answer on page 153.

3. Who set the mark for most passing yards in a Super Bowl . . . and ended up losing the game?
A. Fran Tarkenton
B. John Elway
C. Dan Marino
D. Tom Brady
Answer on page 153.

4. Who has the record for most receiving yards in a Super Bowl?
A. Terrell Owens
B. Jerry Rice
C. Deion Branch
D. Steve Smith Sr.
Answer on page 153.

5. Who was the first defensive player to win Super Bowl MVP?
   A. Ray Nitschke
   B. Bob Lilly
   C. Chuck Howley
   D. Jake Scott
   Answer on page 153.

6. True or False: The Cowboys are one of two teams to have played a Super Bowl in their home stadium.
   Answer on page 153.

7. Former Eagles quarterback Nick Foles is one of two players in NFL history to catch and throw a touchdown pass in the same game. Who is the other player?
   A. David Patten
   B. Jauan Jennings
   C. Darren Sproles
   D. Tom Brady
   Answer on page 153.

8. What two teams played in the highest-scoring Super Bowl?
   A. The San Diego Chargers and San Francisco 49ers
   B. The Dallas Cowboys and Denver Broncos
   C. The New England Patriots and Carolina Panthers
   D. The Kansas City Chiefs and San Francisco 49ers
   Answer on page 153.

9. Does the Lombardi Trophy weigh more or less than 10 pounds?
   Answer on page 154.

10. True or False: Super Bowl I was a sellout.
    Answer on page 154.

11. What is the only Super Bowl matchup that's happened
    three times?
    A. Kansas City Chiefs and San Francisco 49ers
    B. Dallas Cowboys and Miami Dolphins
    C. New England Patriots and New York Giants
    D. Dallas Cowboys and Pittsburgh Steelers
    Answer on page 154.

12. True or False: Tom Brady was the first quarterback to
    start four Super Bowls before turning thirty.
    Answer on page 154.

13. True or False: Madonna was the first female artist to
    headline the Super Bowl halftime show.
    Answer on page 154.

14. Which Super Bowl-winning quarterback also appeared
    on the enemies list of President Richard Nixon?
    A. Bart Starr
    B. Johnny Unitas
    C. Terry Bradshaw
    D. Joe Namath
    Answer on page 154.

15. Why was Super Bowl XLVII interrupted for 34 minutes
    in the second half?
    A. Streakers rushed the field and security struggled to
       bring them down.
    B. The president was late while returning from the

concession stands and the game was held up in
deference to him.
C. The lights went out in the building.
D. A weather-related delay.
Answer on page 154.

16. What show on an alternate network was broadcast
during halftime of the Super Bowl in a bold counter-
programming maneuver designed to make viewers change
the channel?
A. *In Living Color*
B. *Married ... with Children*
C. *Hello, Larry*
D. *The Sopranos*
Answer on page 154.

17. Prince performed "Purple Rain" in the rain during one
memorable halftime performance. What number Super
Bowl did that take place?
A. XLII
B. XXXVI
C. XLI
D. X
Answer on page 154.

18. Who was the first quarterback to win Super Bowls with
two different teams as a starter?
A. Tom Brady
B. Peyton Manning
C. Jim McMahon
D. Drew Brees
Answer on page 154.

19. What year did the NFL begin using Roman numerals to designate each Super Bowl?
    A. 1969
    B. 1971
    C. 1973
    D. 1975
    Answer on page 154.

20. Which two teams have been to the Super Bowl the most times without winning?
    Answer on page 154.

21. Who has the most rushing attempts in a single Super Bowl contest?
    A. John Riggins
    B. Antowain Smith
    C. Marshawn Lynch
    D. Timmy Smith
    Answer on page 155.

22. Who connected for the longest punt in Super Bowl history?
    A. Ray Guy
    B. Bryce Baringer
    C. Kenny Anderson
    D. Johnny Hekker
    Answer on page 155.

23. Who has the longest field goal in Super Bowl history?
    A. Adam Vinatieri
    B. Morten Anderson
    C. Harrison Butker
    D. Kevin Butler
    Answer on page 155.

24. Who had the fewest pass attempts in a single Super Bowl contest?
    A. Brad Johnson
    B. Kerry Collins
    C. Cam Newton
    D. Bob Griese
    Answer on page 155.

25. What team was held to just seven yards rushing in a Super Bowl loss?
    A. Denver Broncos
    B. New England Patriots
    C. Carolina Panthers
    D. Miami Dolphins
    Answer on page 155.

26. Six players have won multiple Defensive Player of the Year awards and have at least one Super Bowl ring. Five of them are in the Hall of Fame. Who is the one who isn't?
    A. Charles Woodson
    B. Michael Strahan
    C. Aaron Donald
    D. Reggie White
    Answer on page 155.

27. What team set the Super Bowl record for most points scored in one quarter?
    A. Washington Redskins
    B. Seattle Seahawks
    C. Green Bay Packers
    D. Kansas City Chiefs
    Answer on page 155.

28. Who holds the Super Bowl record for most interceptions in one contest?
A. Rod Martin
B. Champ Bailey
C. Darrelle Revis
D. Rod Woodson
Answer on page 155.

29. Who is the youngest player to start a Super Bowl?
A. Aaron Hernandez
B. Bryan Bulaga
C. Steve Nicholas
D. Randy Raine
Answer on page 155.

30. True or False: Adam Vinatieri was the oldest player to play in a Super Bowl.
Answer on page 155.

31. True or false: Emmitt Smith has the longest run from scrimmage in Super Bowl history.
Answer on page 155.

32. What future Hall of Fame coach retired immediately after his team's win in Super Bowl II?
A. Bill Walsh
B. Don Shula
C. Paul Brown
D. Vince Lombardi
Answer on page 155.

33. Dallas' Bob Lilly had the greatest sack for a loss (in terms of total yardage) in Super Bowl history. What Super Bowl was it, who was the quarterback, and how many yards did the sack go for?
A. Super Bowl VI, Bob Griese, 29 yards
B. Super Bowl X, Terry Hanratty, 18 yards
C. Super Bowl XII, Craig Morton, 22 yards
D. Super Bowl XIII, Terry Bradshaw, 24 yards
Answer on page 156.

34. True or False: Super Bowl V was the only Super Bowl that saw a member of the losing team win Super Bowl MVP honors.
Answer on page 156.

35. Pittsburgh's Jack Lambert tossed which Dallas player to the ground in a fit of anger in the second half of Super Bowl X?
A. Bob Lilly
B. Herschel Walker
C. Cliff Harris
D. Randy White
Answer on page 156.

36. What was the first Super Bowl played indoors?
A. Super Bowl X
B. Super Bowl XII
C. Super Bowl XXXI
D. Super Bowl XXXVI
Answer on page 156.

37. Which Rams' lineman played Super Bowl XIV on a broken leg?
A. Jackie Slater
B. Fred Dryer
C. Jack Youngblood
D. Vince Ferragamo
Answer on page 156.

38. Super Bowl XIX marked the only appearance in the big game for what future Hall of Fame quarterback?
A. Jim Kelly
B. Drew Bledsoe
C. Ken Anderson
D. Dan Marino
Answer on page 156.

39. What was Phil Simms's completion percentage in Super Bowl XXI against the Broncos?
A. 62 percent
B. 88 percent
C. 95 percent
D. 98 percent
Answer on page 156.

40. Finish this sentence uttered by Joe Montana prior to the game-winning drive against the Bengals in Super Bowl XXIII: "Hey, isn't that _____?"
A. Glenn Close
B. Zsa Zsa Gabor
C. Alice Cooper
D. John Candy
Answer on page 156.

41. Who has the longest kick return in a Super Bowl?
    A. Jacoby Jones
    B. Bethel Johnson
    C. David Guarino
    D. Desmond Howard
    Answer on page 156.

42. Who was the only special teams player to win Super Bowl MVP?
    A. Desmond Howard
    B. Adam Vinatieri
    C. Jacoby Jones
    D. Rodney Martin
    Answer on page 157.

43. Who are the two kickers who tied for the shortest field goal in Super Bowl history?
    A. Adam Vinatieri and Jim Turner
    B. Morten Andersen and Brandon McManus
    C. Jim Turner and Mike Clark
    D. Martin Gramatica and Ross Zapin
    Answer on page 157.

44. Super Bowl VIII was the last NFL game before the league decided to make this decision:
    A. Make face masks and chin straps mandatory.
    B. Move the goal posts to the back of the end zone.
    C. Outlaw defensive kicking.
    D. All of the above.
    Answer on page 157.

45. What non-QB has scored the most points in a Super Bowl?
A. Jason Lefferts
B. Dallas Clark
C. Lynn Swann
D. James White
Answer on page 157.

46. What city has never hosted a Super Bowl?
A. Jacksonville
B. Baltimore
C. Detroit
D. Dallas
Answer on page 157.

47. What city has hosted the most Super Bowls?
A. Los Angeles
B. New Orleans
C. New York
D. Miami
Answer on page 157.

48. True or False: Super Bowl XLVIII at MetLife Stadium in North Jersey had the coldest Super Bowl temperature at kickoff with 34 degrees.
Answer on page 157.

49. Who were the pass-catchers who caught Tom Brady's first and last Super Bowl touchdown tosses?
A. David Patten and Antonio Brown
B. David Patten and Rob Gronkowski
C. Jermaine Wiggins and Mike Evans
D. Troy Brown and Rob Gronkowski
Answer on page 157.

50. Super Bowl XXXVIII featured the longest pass play in Super Bowl history, an 85-yarder. Who was the quarterback and receiver who connected for the record?
A. Tom Brady and Deion Branch
B. Jake Delhomme and Muhsin Muhammad
C. Jake Delhomme and Steve Smith Sr.
D. Tom Brady and David Givens
Answer on page 157.

51. What is Devin Hester's Super Bowl claim to fame?
A. He has the longest kick return for a touchdown in Super Bowl history.
B. He started Super Bowl XLI with a kick return for touchdown.
C. He botched the ceremonial coin toss before Super Bowl XLV.
D. He has the Super Bowl record for most fumbled kickoff returns.
Answer on page 157.

52. The fingertip catch from this Patriots receiver—which took place just inches off the ground—in Super Bowl LI was one of the key plays in New England's second-half comeback.
A. Chris Hogan
B. Malcolm Mitchell
C. Julian Edelman
D. Danny Amendola
Answer on page 157.

53. The combined 16 points in Super Bowl LIII between the Patriots and the Rams made for the lowest-scoring Super Bowl of all- time. How many combined plays were run in the red zone in that game?
A. 0
B. 1
C. 5
D. 10
Answer on page 157.

54. Which one of these head coaches HASN'T won a Super Bowl and a national championship in college?
A. Bill Walsh
B. Jimmy Johnson
C. Pete Carroll
D. Barry Switzer
Answer on page 158.

55. Don McCafferty was the first rookie head coach to win a Super Bowl. As of 2024, who was the most recent to accomplish this feat?
A. Bill Cowher
B. Sean McVay
C. Chuck Noll
D. Jimmy Johnson
Answer on page 158.

56. Who was the oldest coach to win a Super Bowl?
A. Bruce Arians
B. Pete Carroll
C. Tom Coughlin
D. Andy Reid
Answer on page 158.

57. Who scored the first touchdown in Super Bowl history?
A. Mike Merriam
B. Max McGee
C. Ed MacLean
D. Bart Starr
Answer on page 158.

58. Who was the MVP of Super Bowl I?
A. Max McGee
B. Mark Foster
C. Bart Starr
D. Greg Legg
Answer on page 158.

59. What two brothers faced each other in a Super Bowl?
A. Jason and Devon McCourty
B. Clay and Bruce Matthews
C. Jason and Travis Kelce
D. Greg and Darren Levy
Answer on page 158.

60. Which one of these acts has NOT performed at halftime of the Super Bowl?
A. U2
B. Paul McCartney
C. Prince
D. Metallica
Answer on page 158.

61. True or False: Joe Montana was the first player to say "I'm going to Disney World" after winning the Super Bowl.
Answer on page 158.

62. True or False: Super Bowl LI was the first Super Bowl to go to overtime?
Answer on page 158.

63. Who was the first Super Bowl halftime act, and what year did they perform?
A. Elvis Presley, 1968
B. Carol Channing, 1970
C. Paul Revere and the Raiders, 1972
D. Up with People, 1975
Answer on page 158.

64. What four teams have never appeared in a Super Bowl?
Answer on page 158.

65. True or False: The Raiders were the first wild-card team to win a Super Bowl.
Answer on page 158.

66. What bold coaching move did Sean Payton attempt in the second half of Super Bowl XLIV against the Colts?
A. Onside kick
B. A fumblerooski
C. The Statue of Liberty play
D. Fake punt
Answer on page 158.

67. What is David Tyree's claim to Super Bowl fame?
A. He was the streaker who ran on the field during Super Bowl XXXVIII.
B. He delivered the "helmet catch" to help the Giants knock off the Patriots in Super Bowl XLII.

C. He was the Giants' receiver who dumped Gatorade over the head of coach Bill Parcells at the end of Super Bowl XXV.

D. He caught the game-winning touchdown in Super Bowl XLVI to help the Giants beat the Patriots.

Answer on page 159.

68. How many teams have won the Super Bowl after losing the big game the previous year?

A. 3

B. 8

C. 11

D. 13

Answer on page 159.

69. What position has produced the most Super Bowl MVPs?

A. Wide receiver

B. Linebacker

C. Running back

D. Quarterback

Answer on page 159.

Chapter 7

SUPER TRIVIA

ANSWERS

1. 1:F; 2:D; 3:J; 4:B; 5:C; 6:I; 7:E; 8:G; 9:A; 10:H

2. 1:F; 3:J; 3:H; 4:D; 5:B; 6:A; 7:C; 8:E; 9:G; 10:I

3. D—Tom Brady. The future Hall of Famer threw for 505 yards in the Super Bowl LII loss to the Eagles. The game, a 41–33 win for the Eagles, was ultimately decided via a late sack of Brady, who ended up going 28-for-48 in the defeat.

4. B—Jerry Rice. The Hall of Fame receiver had 215 receiving yards in a Super Bowl XXIII win against the Broncos.

5. C—Chuck Howley. He won it for his performance at Super Bowl V in a losing effort with the Cowboys.

6. False. The Buccaneers and the Rams are the only two teams to have played a Super Bowl in their home stadium.

7. B—Jauan Jennings. He did it as a member of the Niners in Super Bowl LVIII.

8. A—The San Diego Chargers and San Francisco 49ers. The two teams combined to score 75 points in Super Bowl XXIX, with San Francisco winning, 49–26.

9. Less. According to the manufacturers, it is roughly seven pounds.

10. False. The inaugural Super Bowl was the only one not to sell out, despite the fact that ticket prices hovered around $12.

11. D—Dallas Cowboys and Pittsburgh Steelers. Pittsburgh and Dallas have met three times, in Super Bowls X (21–17 Cowboys), XIII (35–31 Steelers), and XXX (27–17 Cowboys).

12. False. It was Patrick Mahomes.

13. False. It was Diana Ross, at Super Bowl XXX.

14. D—Joe Namath. The quarterback was among those included on Charles Colson's list of those who were considered political opponents of Nixon.

15. C—The lights went out in the building. A power outage in the Superdome caused a delay in the third quarter of the Niners-Ravens contest.

16. A—*In Living Color*. FOX decided to air a live episode of the sitcom during halftime of Super Bowl XXII.

17. C—XLI. The performance took place at halftime of the Super Bowl between the Colts and Bears, played in Miami.

18. B—Peyton Manning. He won one each with the Colts and Broncos.

19. B—1971. After Super Bowl 4 in 1970, Super Bowl V in 1971 was the first to use roman numerals.

20. Buffalo Bills and Minnesota Vikings, with four appearances each.

21. A—John Riggins. The running back had 38 carries to help lead Washington past Miami in Super Bowl XVII.

22. D—Johnny Hekker. The kicker boomed a 65-yarder for the Rams in Super Bowl LIII.

23. C—Harrison Butker. The kicker delivered a 57-yarder for the Chiefs in Super Bowl LVIII.

24. D—Bob Griese. He attempted just seven passes in the Dolphins' 24–7 win over the Vikings in Super Bowl VIII.

25. B—New England Patriots. New England managed just seven yards on the ground—on 11 rushing attempts—in a 46–10 loss to the Bears in Super Bowl XX.

26. C—Aaron Donald. He's won the award three times, but only retired in early 2024, so it figures it's just a matter of time before he reaches Canton.

27. A—Washington Redskins. The team from DC scored 35 points in the second quarter of its 42–10 win over the Broncos in Super Bowl XXII.

28. A—Rod Martin. The linebacker had three interceptions for the Raiders in their win over the Eagles in Super Bowl XV.

29. B. Bulaga was 21 years, 322 days when he started at offensive tackle for the Packers in Super Bowl XLV.

30. False. It was forty-three-year-old Tom Brady in Super Bowl LV.

31. False. It was 75 yards by Pittsburgh's Willie Parker in Super Bowl XL.

32. D—Vince Lombardi. At the end of the game, he was carried off the field by his players. It was Lombardi's ninth consecutive playoff victory.

33. A—Super Bowl VI, Bob Griese, 29 yards.

34. True. Chuck Howley of the Cowboys won the award, but Dallas ended up losing to Baltimore.

35. C. Cliff Harris. Lambert was incensed after Harris taunted the Pittsburgh kicker after a miss. After the game, Lambert was asked about his incident, and said, "We're the Pittsburgh Steelers. We're supposed to be the intimidators."

36. B—Super Bowl XII. Played at the Louisiana Superdome, it was the first Super Bowl played indoors. Dallas beat Denver, 27–10.

37. C—Jack Youngblood. Turns out, it was later revealed Youngblood played the entire postseason—and the Pro Bowl—with the injury. When he was asked why he didn't beg out of the Pro Bowl because of it, he reportedly replied, "Everybody asked me when we got to Hawaii, 'What the heck are you doing here? You've got a broken tibia,'" Youngblood told CBS Sports. "I said, 'Shut up, I'm not going to miss this party.'"

38. D—Dan Marino. The Hall of Fame quarterback's only Super Bowl appearance saw his Dolphins fall to Joe Montana and the Niners.

39. B—88 percent. He was named Super Bowl MVP in New York's win over Denver.

40. D—John Candy. According to teammate Harris Barton, Montana noticed the star of *Planes, Trains, and Automobiles* on the sidelines as he entered the huddle prior to the game-winning drive to beat the Bengals.

41. A—Jacoby Jones. The wide receiver went for 108 yards for Baltimore in Super Bowl XLVII.

42. A—Desmond Howard. The former Heisman Trophy winner took home the honors for his performance in Super Bowl XXXI, which included a key kick return in the Green Bay win over New England.

43. C—Jim Turner and Mike Clark. The two kickers tied with nine-yard field goals—both delivered when the uprights were on the goal line. They were moved back in 1974, so this is a record that can never be broken.

44. B—Move the goal posts to the back of the end zone.

45. D—James White. The Patriots running back scored 20 points in Super Bowl LI, including the game-winning touchdown in overtime.

46. B—Baltimore.

47. D—Miami. As of 2024, the Florida city has hosted the game eleven times.

48. False. Super Bowl VI in New Orleans had a kickoff temperature of 39 degrees Fahrenheit.

49. A—David Patten and Antonio Brown.

50. B—Jake Delhomme and Muhsin Muhammad. The Carolina connection pulled off the feat during their Super Bowl XXXVIII loss to New England.

51. B. He started Super Bowl XLI with a kick return for touchdown. It was the first time in Super Bowl history that had happened.

52. C—Julian Edelman. For that catch, and the rest of his efforts that afternoon, he was named Super Bowl MVP.

53. B—1.

54. A—Bill Walsh.

55. A—Bill Cowher. The rookie head coach led the Pittsburgh Steelers to victory in Super Bowl XL over the Seattle Seahawks, 21–10.

56. A—Bruce Arians. The coach was 68 years and 127 days when he led the Bucs to victory in Super Bowl LV.

57. B. Max McGee. The receiver scored on a 37-yard pass from Bart Starr in the first quarter of Super Bowl I.

58. C—Bart Starr. The Hall of Fame quarterback threw for 250 yards and two touchdowns on the day.

59. C—Jason and Travis Kelce. Jason, an offensive lineman for the Eagles, and Travis, a tight end for the Chiefs, faced each other in Super Bowl LVII.

60. D—Metallica.

61. False. It was Phil Simms after Super Bowl XXI.

62. True: The Patriots beat the Falcons.

63. B—Carol Channing (1970). She was the first celebrity performer for a Super Bowl halftime show in 1970 when the Kansas City Chiefs beat the Minnesota Vikings, 23–7, at Tulane Stadium in New Orleans.

64. Detroit Lions, Jacksonville Jaguars, Cleveland Browns, and Houston Texans.

65. True. They beat the Eagles, 27–10, to win Super Bowl XV.

66. A—Onside lick. Payton called for an onside kick at the start of the third quarter in the 31–17 win.

67. B. He delivered the "helmet catch" to help the Giants knock off the Patriots in Super Bowl XLII.

68. A—3. Only the 1971 Cowboys, 1972 Dolphins, and 2018 Patriots were able to hoist the Lombardi Trophy a year after being on the short end of the Super Bowl scoreboard.

69. D—Quarterback. On thirty-three occasions, the quarterback has been named Super Bowl MVP.

Chapter 8

SAY WHAT?

The NFL is filled with colorful characters who say some wild things. Fill in the blanks and reveal the speaker of some of the greatest quotes in recent NFL history:

1. "That is a _____ act by Randy Moss."
   Answer on page 165.

2. "If me and King Kong went into an alley, only one of us would come out, and it wouldn't be the _____."
   Answer on page 165.

3. "We didn't have steroids. If I wanted to get pumped, I had to _____."
   Answer on page 165.

4. "He couldn't spell _____ if you gave him the C and the T."
   Answer on page 165.

5. "Getcha _____ ready."
   Answer on page 165.

6. "The Vikings got _____. The Cowboys got nothing more than a huge handful of Minnesota smoke. And who knows if there'll ever be any fire."
   Answer on page 165–166.

7. "_____ is the next Brett Favre."
   Answer on page 166.

8. "We saw a weak team. The _____, let's face it, they're not good anymore."
Answer on page 166.

9. "With Larry Shannon coming to our football team by the way, he's probably a step faster than _____. So he's bigger, he's taller, he's faster. Sometimes everybody gets all carried away, for instance, with _____ and I don't want to be talking about somebody else's player. I'm just going to make an example. Some of these people get so carried away. I'd like to pull them aside and say, how many films did you grade in coming to your evaluation?
Answer on page 166.

10. "I love _____ some _____!"
Answer on page 166.

11. "If you look _____, you feel _____, If you feel _____, you play _____, If you play _____, they pay _____."
Answer on page 166.

12. "If_____ is not a successful quarterback in the NFL, I'm done. That's it. I'm out."
Answer on page 166.

13. "I feel sorry for the poor guy who is going to buy the _____. It's a no-win situation for him, because if he wins, well, so what, they've won through the years, and if he loses, which seems likely because they're having troubles, he'll be known to the world as a loser."
Answer on page 167.

14. "_____ up, son. _____ up."
Answer on page 167.

15. "When you're rich, you don't write checks. _____ _____, homey."
Answer on page 167.

16. "We're talking about our _____ kicker who got liquored up and ran his mouth off."
    Answer on page 167.

17. "When you try me with a sorry receiver like _____."
    Answer on page 167.

18. "We want the ball and we're gonna _____."
    Answer on page 167.

19. "You _____, bro?"
    Answer on page 167.

20. "Do your _____."
    Answer on page 167.

21. "You've been watching _____ too, huh? That's cool. Watch this."
    Answer on page 168.

22. "I'm just here so I don't get _____."
    Answer on page 168.

23. "Yo soy _____."
    Answer on page 168.

24. "Let's go out there like a bunch of _____."
    Answer on page 168.

25. "I'm bored. I'm broke. I'm _____."
    Answer on page 168.

26. "I've eaten _____ bigger than you."
    Answer on page 168.

27. "There are three things in life's that's certain: Death, taxes, and _____ will always be open."
    Answer on page 168.

28. "All he does is talk. He's _____, and you can print that. I was happy when he was in the game."
Answer on page 168.

29. "Mr. President, we need the National Guard, we need as many men as you can spare because we are killing the _____!"
Answer on page 168–169.

30. "The _____ are who we thought they were! That's why we took the damn field! If you want to crown them, then crown their asses. But they are who we thought they were, and we let 'em off the hook!"
Answer on page 169.

31. "This is what's great about sports. You _____ to win the game. Hello? You _____ to win the game. You don't _____ to just _____ it."
Answer on page 169.

32. "Uh, _____? _____? Don't talk to me about _____! You kidding me? _____? I just hope we can win another game."
Answer on page 169.

33. "We couldn't do _____ offensively."
Answer on page 169.

34. "We're only going to score _____ points? Ha ha ha! OK. Is Plax playing defense?"
Answer on page 169.

35. "Nobody in football should be called a genius. A genius is a guy like _____."
Answer on page 169.

36. "Just _____ and _____."
Answer on page 169.

Chapter 8

SAY WHAT?

ANSWERS

1. "That is a **disgusting** act by Randy Moss." (Broadcaster Joe Buck, describing the action as the former Minnesota receiver pretended to pull down his pants and moon the crowd at Lambeau Field.)

2. "If me and King Kong went into an alley, only one of us would come out, and it wouldn't be the **monkey**." (Lyle Alzado, on his playing style.)

3. "We didn't have steroids. If I wanted to get pumped, I had to **drink a case of beer**." (Baltimore defensive lineman Art Donovan, talking about "performance enhancers" in the 1950s.)

4. "He couldn't spell **cat** if you gave him the C and the T." (Thomas Henderson, talking about Terry Bradshaw prior to Super Bowl XIII.)

5. "Getcha **popcorn** ready." (A message to the media from Terrell Owens prior to a 2007 game between the Patriots and Cowboys.)

6. "The Vikings got **Hershel Walker**. The Cowboys got nothing more than a huge handful of Minnesota smoke. And who

knows if there'll ever be any fire." (*Dallas Morning News* columnist Randy Galloway on the trade that sent Herschel Walker from Dallas to Minnesota. The deal helped set the stage for the Cowboys' three titles in four years.)

7. "**Tim Tebow** is the next Brett Favre." (Skip Bayless, on ESPN's *First Take*, January 2009.)

8. "We saw a weak team. The **New England Patriots**, let's face it, they're not good anymore." (Analyst and former QB Trent Dilfer on ESPN in 2014, talking about the Patriots, who would go on to win the Super Bowl later that season.)

9. "With Larry Shannon coming to our football team by the way, he's probably a step faster than **Randy Moss**. So he's bigger, he's taller, he's faster. Sometimes everybody gets all carried away, for instance, with **Moss** and I don't want to be talking about somebody else's player. I'm just going to make an example. Some of these people get so carried away. I'd like to pull them aside and say, how many films did you grade in coming to your evaluation?" (Miami coach Jimmy Johnson after the Dolphins drafted Larry Shannon instead of Randy Moss in 1998.)

10. "I love **me** some **me**!" (Terrell Owens, on the sideline after a spectacular reception.)

11. "If you look **good**, you feel **good**, If you feel **good**, you play **good**, If you play **good**, they pay **good**." (Deion Sanders, on his philosophy.)

12. "If **Jimmy Clausen** is not a successful quarterback in the NFL, I'm done. That's it. I'm out." (Draft analyst Mel Kiper Jr. on ESPN in 2010, talking about Notre Dame quarterback Jimmy Clausen.)

13. "I feel sorry for the poor guy who is going to buy the **Dallas Cowboys**. It's a no-win situation for him, because if he wins, well, so what, they've won through the years, and if he loses, which seems likely because they're having troubles, he'll be known to the world as a loser." (Donald Trump, speaking with the *New York Times* in 1984. The Cowboys are now the richest franchise in the NFL.)

14. "**Ice** up, son. **Ice** up." (Panthers wide receiver Steve Smith Sr., to New England cornerback Aqib Talib, after a 2013 win over the Patriots.)

15. "When you're rich, you don't write checks. **Straight cash**, homey." (Randy Moss, explaining to the media in January 2005 how he pays his fines.)

16. "We're talking about our **idiot** kicker who got liquored up and ran his mouth off." (Peyton Manning, speaking with reporters in 2003 about comments from Indianapolis kicker Mike Vanderjagt's comments.)

17. "When you try me with a sorry receiver like [**Michael**] **Crabtree**, that's the result you're going to get! Don't you ever talk about me!" (Richard Sherman to Erin Andrews after the Seahawks beat the Niners in the 2013 NFC Championship Game.)

18. "We want the ball and we're gonna **score**." (Seahawks quarterback Matt Hasselbeck at the start of overtime in a 2004 playoff game against Green Bay. Shortly after his declaration, Hasselbeck threw a pick six, and Seattle lost the game.)

19. "You **mad**, bro?" (Richard Sherman to Tom Brady after Seattle beat New England in 2012.)

20. "Do your **job**." (Bill Belichick, offering up the Patriots' mantra for two decades.)

21. "You've been watching **film** too, huh? That's cool. Watch this." (Cam Newton to Green Bay defenders in 2017, caught on the field right before he tossed a touchdown pass.)

22. "I'm just here so I don't get **fined**." (A reluctant Marshawn Lynch, speaking with reporters during the run-up to Super Bowl XLIX.)

23. "Yo soy **fiesta**." (Rob Gronkowski, speaking with Spanish reporters while he was a tight end with the Patriots.)

24. "Let's go out there like a bunch of **crazed dogs**." (Lawrence Taylor, caught on the sidelines by NFL Films, exhorting his defensive teammates.)

25. "I'm bored. I'm broke. I'm **back**." (John Riggins, in 1981, explaining why he returned to football after sitting out the 1980 season because of a contract dispute.)

26. I've eaten **burritos** bigger than you." (Houston's J. J. Watt, caught mic'd up by NFL Films, talking trash to diminutive Baltimore running back Ray Rice.)

27. "There are three things in life's that's certain: Death, taxes, and **85** will always be open." (Chad "Ochocinco" Johnson, speaking with the media about his skills.)

28. "All he does is talk. He's **terrible**, and you can print that. I was happy when he was in the game." (Bill Belichick, speaking with the media after Super Bowl XXXIX about Philadelphia receiver Freddie Mitchell. The wide receiver would have one catch for 11 yards in the game.)

29. "Mr. President, we need the National Guard, we need as many men as you can spare because we are killing the **Patriots**!" (Denver tight end Shannon Sharpe, caught on camera by NFL

Films during a blowout win in 1996 against the New England Patriots.)

30. "The **Bears** are who we thought they were! That's why we took the damn field! If you want to crown them, then crown their asses. But they are who we thought they were, and we let 'em off the hook!" (Arizona head coach Dennis Green after a narrow loss to Chicago in 2006.)

31. "This is what's great about sports. You **play** to win the game. Hello? You **play** to win the game. You don't **play** to just **play** it." (Jets coach Herm Edwards, in a 2002 press conference.)

32. "Uh, **playoffs**? **Playoffs**? Don't talk to me about **playoffs**! You kidding me? **Playoffs**? I just hope we can win another game." (Colts coach Jim Mora in a 2001 press conference, after being asked about his team's postseason chances following a loss.)

33. "We couldn't do **diddly-poo** offensively." (Saints coach Jim Mora, speaking with reporters after a 1996 game where his team's offense was ineffective in defeat.)

34. "We're only going to score **17** points? Hahaha, okay. It Plax playing defense?" (Tom Brady before Super Bowl XLII, when asked about Plaxico Burress's prediction the Giants were going to win, 23–17. New England's record-setting offense scored 14 in the loss.)

35. "Nobody in football should be called a genius. A genius is a guy like **Norman Einstein**." (Quarterback Joe Theismann, talking about knowledge and the game of pro football.)

36. "Just **Benjamin** and **Franklin**." (Former Seattle defensive lineman Michael Bennett talking about his friends in the NFL.)

Chapter 9

HATERS GONNA HATE

Do you have an annoying Eagles fan in your life? How about an uncle who won't shut up about the Seahawks? Or maybe a brother who won't stop bragging about the Chiefs? Then this chapter is for you. If you need ammunition to help silence another fan, check out these questions that focus on some of the most memorable gaffes in league history. "Oh yeah? Well, at least my team didn't (fill in the blank)!" Use 'em to help silence that know-it-all pal of yours—and feel free to conveniently skip over the ones that detail the biggest mistakes made by your own team.

1. Match the team with their memorable gaffe.
    1. The Butt Fumble   A. Cleveland Browns
    2. Garo's Gaffe   B. New York Giants
    3. The Wrong Way Run   C. New York Jets
    4. The Fumble   D. Minnesota Vikings
    5. The Miracle at the Meadowlands E. Miami Dolphins
    Answer on page 189.

171

2. This Colts coach was so brutal, his reputation *played a part* in making John Elway initially choose a career in baseball so as to avoid being taken first in the draft by Baltimore.
A. Tony Dungy
B. Ted Marchibroda
C. Frank Kush
D. Moe Green
Answer on page 189.

3. Which Bears kicker missed what would have been a game-winning field goal in a 2018 wild-card playoff game against the Eagles?
A. Kevin Butler
B. Cody Parkey
C. Robbie Gould
D. Nick Folk
Answer on page 189–190.

4. What Chicago quarterback got the Bears all the way to the 2010 NFC Championship Game, but suffered a knee injury that set the stage for a Green Bay win?
A. Kyle Orton
B. Jay Cutler
C. Doug Flutie
D. Nick Foles
Answer on page 190.

5. This former Heisman Trophy winner was the starting quarterback for the Tampa Bay Buccaneers in their first season, but went 0–12 as a starter.
A. Steve Spurrier

B. Jim Plunkett
C. Roger Staubach
D. Paul Hornung
Answer on page 190.

6. The Buccaneers drafted Bo Jackson first overall in 1986, but he never played a game for Tampa Bay. Did the Bucs ever get any compensation for losing out on Jackson?
Answer on page 190.

7. What Houston quarterback set an NFL record by throwing pick sixes in four straight games?
A. Matt Schaub
B. Brock Osweiler
C. David Carr
D. Scott Zolak
Answer on page 190.

8. What did Lin Elliott do to deserve a place in Chiefs infamy?
A. He was the GM who drafted Todd Blackledge ahead of Dan Marino.
B. Fumbled three times in a playoff defeat against the Patriots.
C. Missed three field goals from 42 yards or less in a playoff loss to the Colts in 1995.
D. He was the defensive coordinator for the worst loss in franchise history.
Answer on page 190.

9. Buffalo running back Thurman Thomas couldn't find this key piece of equipment prior to the start of Super Bowl XXVI, causing him to miss the first play of the game.
   A. Jockstrap
   B. Mouthpiece
   C. Helmet
   D. Shoelaces
   Answer on page 191.

10. What Jacksonville punter swung an axe and hit his own foot in 2003?
    A. Ken Walter
    B. Bryce Baringer
    C. Josh Scobee
    D. Chris Hanson
    Answer on page 191.

11. This Detroit quarterback ran out of the back of the end zone to avoid the pass rush, taking a safety in the process.
    A. Sam Bradford
    B. Eric Hipple
    C. Jared Goff
    D. Dan Orlovsky
    Answer on page 191.

12. What was the nickname given to the touchdown at the end of the game between the Packers and Seahawks in 2012 that resulted in one replacement ref signaling for a touchdown and another waving it off as incomplete?
    A. The Fail Mary
    B. No Dice

C. Aaron's Remorse
D. None of the above
Answer on page 191.

13. Which Dallas lineman inadvertently slid into the football in a 1993 game after a missed Cowboys field goal attempt late in the contest, ultimately setting the stage for a Miami win?
A. Nate Newton
B. Leon Lett
C. Charles Haley
D. Barry Abercrombie
Answer on page 192.

14. What Philadelphia receiver's premature celebration before crossing the goal line in a 2008 game against Dallas negated a touchdown?
A. Terrell Owens
B. Greg Lewis
C. Freddie Jackson
D. DeSean Jackson
Answer on page 192.

15. Which Tampa Bay receiver stripped to the waist in the middle of the 2022 game and walked off the field, waving to fans on the way to the locker room?
A. Mike Evans
B. Antonio Brown
C. Tee Higgins
D. Joe Jurevicius
Answer on page 192.

16. Who was the Indianapolis punter who had a hand in trying to execute a fake punt against the Patriots in 2015 that went horribly wrong?
A. Hunter Smith
B. Mike Vanderjagt
C. Pat McAfee
D. Chick Magee
Answer on page 192.

17. Late in a 2023 regular-season contest, this Kansas City pass catcher was offsides, negating what would have been a touchdown for the Chiefs.
A. Marquez Valdes-Scantling
B. Tyreek Hill
C. Kadarius Toney
D. Travis Kelce
Answer on page 192–193.

18. True or False: The Vikings have appeared in four Super Bowl games, but have only led at any point in one of them.
Answer on page 193.

19. Who was the head coach of the Falcons that blew a 28–3 lead in Super Bowl LI against the Patriots?
A. Dan Reeves
B. Jerry Glanville
C. Arthur Smith
D. Dan Quinn
Answer on page 193.

20. How many times was Tom Brady sacked in the regular
season over the course of his career?
A. Between 150 and 200 times
B. Between 201 and 250 times
C. Between 251 and 300 times
D. More than 300 times
Answer on page 193.

21. What was the name of the Chiefs defender who crashed
into Tom Brady's knee in the 2008 opener, leaving him
sidelined for the rest of the season?
A. Bernard Pollard
B. Bernard McGuirk
C. Scot Pollard
D. Greg Petronzio
Answer on page 193.

22. What color hoodie did Bill Belichick wear in New Eng-
land's infamous Super Bowl XLII loss to the Giants?
A. Striped
B. Red
C. White
D. Black
Answer on page 193.

23. In the 2002 NFC wild-card contest between the Giants
and Niners, New York took a 38–14 second-half lead.
Which San Francisco quarterback led the Niners back to
beat New York?
A. Steve Young
B. Steve Bono
C. Stephen Popper
D. Jeff Garcia
Answer on page 193–194.

24. Jimmy Johnson's last game as a head coach of the Dolphins was a 62–7 playoff loss to what team?
A. New England Patriots
B. New York Jets
C. Buffalo Bills
D. Jacksonville Jaguars
Answer on page 194.

25. What was the name of the former New England assistant coach who blew the whistle on the Patriots, sparking the "Spygate" scandal?
A. Charlie Weis
B. Matt Patricia
C. Eric Mangini
D. Romeo Crennel
Answer on page 194.

26. Who was the name of the Seattle player who was the intended target of Russell Wilson's pass attempt that was picked off by Malcolm Butler at the end of Super Bowl XLIX?
A. Doug Baldwin
B. Ricardo Lockette
C. Marshawn Lynch
D. Steve Largent
Answer on page 194.

27. Which franchise suffered the worst loss—by point differential—in the history of the NFL?
A. Green Bay Packers
B. Chicago Bears
C. Dallas Cowboys

D. Washington Redskins
Answer on page 194.

28. What coach indirectly praised the 9/11 hijackers during a team meeting in 2019, citing them as a model when it came to sticking together?
A. Sean McDermott
B. Adam Gase
C. Pete Carroll
D. Doug Marrone
Answer on page 194.

29. What opponent delivered the worst loss (by point differential) in Cowboys history?
A. New York Giants
B. Philadelphia Eagles
C. New England Patriots
D. Chicago Bears
Answer on page 194.

30. Which team dealt Tom Brady his final loss as a member of the Patriots during the 2019 playoffs?
A. Jacksonville Jaguars
B. Tennessee Titans
C. Indianapolis Colts
D. Houston Texans
Answer on page 194.

31. From 2000 through 2023, the Patriots had one head coach in Bill Belichick. How many different head coaches (including interim) did the Dolphins have in that same stretch?

A. Five
B. Eight
C. Eleven
D. Thirteen

Answer on page 195.

32. Which Browns running back fumbled on the goal line late in the 1987 AFC Championship Game against the Broncos?

A. Earnest Byner
B. Mike Cloud
C. Randall Floyd
D. Kevin Mack

Answer on page 195.

33. What team came back from a 12-point deficit late in the fourth quarter of the 2014 NFC Championship Game to beat the Packers and advance to the Super Bowl?

A. Carolina Panthers
B. Seattle Seahawks
C. New York Giants
D. San Francisco 49ers

Answer on page 195.

34. Which quarterback committed six turnovers on the way to "leading" his team to a 49–15 loss in the 2015 NFC Championship Game?

A. Carson Palmer

B. Cam Newton
C. Peyton Manning
D. Kirk Cousins
Answer on page 195.

35. What was the name of the Buffalo kicker whose field-goal attempt went wide right near the end of Super Bowl XXV?
A. Carlos Huerta
B. Scott Norwood
C. Matt Bahr
D. Steve Tasker
Answer on page 195.

36. What was the name of the Dallas player who mishandled the snap on a field-goal attempt that led to a 2006 playoff loss against the Seahawks?
A. Drew Henson
B. Troy Aikman
C. Tony Romo
D. Jay Novacek
Answer on page 195.

37. What was the only team in NFL history to start the season 9–2 and miss the playoffs?
A. 1993 Miami Dolphins
B. 1989 San Diego Chargers
C. 1979 Pittsburgh Steelers
D. 1976 Kansas City Chiefs
Answer on page 195–196.

38. Which team saw their roof collapse under the weight of snow during the 2010 season, forcing them to find alternate facilities at a nearby university?
A. Minnesota Vikings
B. New Orleans Saints
C. Detroit Lions
D. New York Jets
Answer on page 196.

39. What was the name of the Minnesota player on the receiving end of the Minneapolis Miracle, a last-second touchdown catch that knocked New Orleans out of the 2017 postseason?
A. Justin Jefferson
B. Adam Thielen
C. Cris Carter
D. Stefon Diggs
Answer on page 196.

40. What was the name of the kit that helped generate synthetic urine that Minnesota running back Onterrio Smith used to try and beat an NFL drug test in 2005?
A. Fakepee.com
B. Whizzinator
C. Drugstore Cowboy
D. The Whizz Palace
Answer on page 196.

41. What did Bryan Cox do before a game against the Bills in Buffalo that caused him to eventually be fined by the league?
A. Drove a beer truck onto the field and sprayed beer at the officials.

B. Spit on officials.
C. Flipped double-birds to the crowd.
D. Fought Buffalo quarterback Jim Kelly.
Answer on page 196–197.

42. Which coach was investigated in 2005 for organizing and profiting from a Super Bowl ticket-scalping operation?
A. Mike Tice
B. Andy Reid
C. Dennis Green
D. Buddy Ryan
Answer on page 197.

43. What was the name of the New York receiver whose touchdown catch near the end of Super Bowl XLII helped ruin the Patriots' unbeaten season?
A. Plaxico Burress
B. Victor Cruz
C. David Tyree
D. Brandon Jacobs
Answer on page 197.

44. What Raiders quarterback threw five interceptions in the Super Bowl XXXVII loss to the Buccaneers?
A. Ken Stabler
B. Rich Gannon
C. JaMarcus Russell
D. Randall Cunningham
Answer on page 197.

45. After winning the Bart Starr Award—given to a player who exemplified high moral character—in the days before Super Bowl XXXIII, what happened to Atlanta defensive back Eugene Robinson?
A. Arrested on drug charges.
B. Predicted a Falcons' blowout win.
C. Asked to sing the national anthem before the game.
D. Arrested for soliciting a prostitute who turned out to be an undercover cop.
Answer on page 197.

46. Who were the two Oilers coaches that ended up tangling with each other during a 1993 game?
A. Bum Phillips and Wade Phillips
B. Jerry Glanville and Jack Pardee
C. Buddy Ryan and Kevin Gilbride
D. Hank Ketchum and Buddy Ryan
Answer on page 197.

47. What season did the Oilers blow a 35–3 lead to the Bills in a playoff game in Buffalo?
A. 1990
B. 1992
C. 1993
D. 1994
Answer on page 198.

48. Match the owner with his reported indiscretion
1. David Tepper   A. Giving the middle finger to fans
2. Bud Adams   B. Sexual and racial harassment
3. Jerry Richardson C. Throwing a drink on fans
4. Jimmy Haslam   D. Guilty of racketeering
5. Zygi Wilf   E. Fraud
Answer on page 198.

49. Which owner did NOT preside over a team move?
A. Stan Kroenke
B. Robert Irsay
C. Art Modell
D. Mark Davis
Answer on page 198.

50. In a 2013 AFC wild-card game, Andy Reid and the Chiefs blew a 38–10 second-half lead and lost to what team?
A. Indianapolis Colts
B. New England Patriots
C. Baltimore Ravens
D. Buffalo Bills
Answer on page 198.

51. Who was the head coach of the Lions during their disastrous 2008 season that saw their season finish with an 0–16 record?
A. John Robinson
B. Dan Campbell
C. Chuck Schick
D. Rod Marinelli
Answer on page 198.

52. Which team dealt the Broncos the worst loss in franchise history (by point differential) in 2023.
A. Las Vegas Raiders
B. San Francisco 49ers
C. Philadelphia Eagles
D. Miami Dolphins
Answer on page 198.

53. What tight end dropped a surefire touchdown catch for the Cowboys in the second half of Super Bowl XIII that might have given Dallas the win?
A. Jay Novacek
B. Jackie Smith
C. Rob Coates
D. Heath Miller
Answer on page 198.

54. What team took quarterback Kelly Stouffer sixth overall in the 1987 draft, only to see him sit out the entire season because of a contract dispute?
A. Atlanta Falcons
B. St. Louis Cardinals
C. New England Patriots
D. Minnesota Vikings
Answer on page 198–199.

55. What team beat the Eagles in the Fog Bowl?
A. Chicago Bears
B. New Orleans Saints
C. Dallas Cowboys
D. Los Angeles Rams
Answer on page 199.

56. Which team passed up the chance to sign future Super Bowl champion Drew Brees prior to the 2006 season in favor of Daunte Culpepper?
A. Chicago Bears
B. Dallas Cowboys
C. Miami Dolphins
D. New Orleans Saints
Answer on page 199.

57. Which team's play was so bad in 1980 that fans started wearing bags over their heads at games?
    A. Cincinnati Bengals
    B. Buffalo Bills
    C. Chicago Bears
    D. New Orleans Saints
    Answer on page 199.

58. What San Francisco running back fumbled late in the 1990 NFC Championship Game, opening the door for a comeback by the New York Giants?
    A. Rickey Watters
    B. Roger Craig
    C. Norby Williamson
    D. Andre Reese
    Answer on page 199–200.

59. What team completed a fourth-quarter comeback against San Francisco in a 1972 playoff game, rebounding from a 28–13 deficit at the start of the fourth quarter to pull off the shocker?
    A. New York Giants
    B. Los Angeles Rams
    C. Dallas Cowboys
    D. Chicago Bears
    Answer on page 200.

60. Which Cincinnati player took a late unnecessary roughness penalty in a 2015 playoff game against Pittsburgh that allowed the Steelers to complete a remarkable comeback win?
A. Vontaze Burfict
B. Chad Johnson
C. Gio Bernard
D. Ickey Woods
Answer on page 200.

Chapter 9

HATERS GONNA HATE

ANSWERS

1. 1:C; 2:E; 3:D; 4:A; 5: B

2. B—Frank Kush. During his more than twenty years as the head coach at Arizona State University, Kush built a reputation as being not only physically demanding toward his players, but both physically and mentally abusive as well (and was later fired by the school due to such behaviors, which included a lawsuit brought against the school by a former player). In 1982—the year before Elway was drafted—the Colts and Kush went 0–8–1 in a strike-shortened season. After one more season in Baltimore (in which the team went 7–9, which was Elway's rookie season), on March 28-29, the Colts initiated the "late night move," with the franchise becoming the Indianapolis Colts.

3. C—Cody Parkey. After the Eagles took a 16–15 lead with 56 seconds left in regulation, the Bears needed a miracle. After a 58-yard return by Tarik Cohen and two big catches by Allen Robinson, the Bears had the ball on the Eagles 25-yard line with just 10 seconds left on the clock. After the Eagles called time out just before Parkey's 43-yard attempt (which was successful), the teams lined up again for what would be the game-deciding play. Already hitting three field goals on the day, Parkey lined up and kicked the ball…which began veering and bounced off the left upright *and* the crossbar (or what announcer Cris Collinsworth called a "double doink"), then falling in front of the end zone. No good. The Eagles would go on to win the Super Bowl.

4. B—Jay Cutler. After taking a sack late in the first half, Cutler appeared in one series in the third quarter before being removed from the game. Though questioned by many, it was later revealed that he had sustained a Grade 2 MCL sprain. While his replacement, Caleb Hanie, put together a terrific performance to get the Bears back into the game, the Packers would end up victories, 21–14.

5. A—Steve Spurrier. Known more for his success as a college coach, Spurrier (who had been a star at the University of Florida—a school he would later coach) joined the Bucs after nine years with the 49ers, in which he started just 26 games, going 13–24–1. He would start 12 of the team's 14 games, going 0–12 and being released at the end of the season.

6. No. As Jackson did not play in the NFL that season (instead playing for baseball's Kansas City Royals), he saw his rights go back into the draft. He was then drafted in the seventh round by the Los Angeles Raiders the following year.

7. A—Matt Schaub. After six seasons as the starter for the Texans (going 44–36), Schaub would throw INTs against the Titans, Ravens, Seahawks, and 49ers in consecutive games. To no surprise, 2013 would be his last season in Houston.

8. C—Elliott missed three field goals from 42 yards or less in a playoff loss to the Colts in 1995, after the team went 13–3 on the season and received a first-round bye. Again, to no surprise, 1995 would be his last season in Kansas City (and in the NFL).

9. C—Helmet. Missing the Bills' first offensive series, the missing helmet was shortly found . . . on the defensive end of the bench! Perhaps a defensive player had mistakenly picked it up, but even after its retrieval Thomas was unable to help his team beat the Redskins.

10. D—Chris Hanson. First-year head coach Jack Del Rio had placed an axe in the team's locker room as a motivational tool ("keep chopping wood"). But when the team's punter, Chris Hanson, went to give it a swing, the axe bounced off the stump and ended up in his lower right leg. "I'll find another slogan," said Del Rio after the "ax-cident."

11. D—Dan Orlovsky. In a season in which the Lions finished 0–16, Orlovsky's moment is close to the top of the list of unforgettable moments. In the first quarter of their Week 14 game against the Vikings, with the ball on their own 1-yard line, Orlovsky scrambled in the end zone to avoid pressure from lineman Jared Allen. While almost immediately stepping out of the end zone, he kept scrambling, looking for a target . . . and kept scrambling . . . and kept scrambling. The pay would (obviously) result in a safety, and the Lions would lose, 20–16.

12. A—The Fail Mary. Also known as the "Inaccurate Reception," a "catch" by Golden Tate was ruled as a touchdown by one ref and an incompletion by another. While the replacement refs would end up calling it a TD and giving the Seahawks a 14–12 win, the league would later state that offensive passing interference should have been called on Tate, which would have ended the game in the Packers' favor. Two days later, the league and the refs came to an agreement, and the replacement refs we sent on their way.

13. B—Leon Lett. The two-time Pro Bowler made this faux pas on Thanksgiving Day against the Dolphins. After a teammate had blocked a potential game-winning field goal Miami, Lett—instead of doing *nothing*—decided to try and recover the ball. He failed, and the Dolphins were able to jump on the ball and recover. They would kick the game-winning field goal, stealing the game, 16–14.

14. D—DeSean Jackson. After the flashy rookie caught what seemed like a 60-yard touchdown pass from quarterback Donovan McNabb, he threw the ball behind him in celebration . . . only he did so on the 1-yard line. After review, the ball was given to Philly just outside the end zone (as it had not been picked up by a Cowboy player), and Brian Westbrook ran it in for a touchdown. In a crazy back-and-forth game, the Cowboys would end up victories, 41–37.

15. B—Antonio Brown. In the third quarter of a game against the Jets, the much-maligned wide receiver removed his pads, took off his shirt and threw it into the stands, and danced/waved at the New York crowd before exiting the field. He would be released days after the incident.

16. C—Pat McAfee. In an unusual formation, McAfee lined up under center and took the snap. The issue was that the Colts line had completely shifted, leaving the punter unprotected. The play didn't work (obviously), and the Pats went on to win, 34–27.

17. C—Kadarius Toney. With the Chefs trailing the Bills, 20–17, with just over a minute left in regulations, Patrick Mahomes hit tight end Travis Kelce for what looked to be a 30-yard reception—until he threw the ball backwards to Toney, who ran it in for a touchdown. However, Toney had lined up offsides, and so what would have been a trick play for the ages was called back. The Chiefs would fail to score on the drive and lose to Buffalo.

18. False. They have never led in *any* of the four Super Bowls in which they have appeared, losing by a combined score of 95–34.

19. D—Dan Quinn. After the infamous Super Bowl collapse, Quinn would go on to have just one more winning season in Atlanta before being dismissed during the 2020 season.

20. D—More than 300 times—for a total of 565 career sacks (five behind the all-time leader, Fran Tarkenton). However, of the 80 quarterbacks with at least 150 games played, he had the fifth-lowest sack percentage (percentage of times sacked when attempting to pass), at 4.48.

21. A—Bernard Pollard. Coming off an MVP season, Brady was taken out in the first quarter of the first game of the season. After the season, the "Brady Rule" was created, prohibiting defensive players who are on the ground from lunging at a quarterback's legs.

22. B—Red. Historically, Belichick usually went with a gray or blue hoodie, but chose red for that contest (a decision he most likely regrets, depending on how superstitious he is).

23. D—Jeff Garcia. Scoring 25 straight points, the 49ers held a one-point lead with six seconds remaining on the clock. With the Giants lined up for a 41-yard field goal that would have won the game, the snap couldn't be controlled by the holder, Matt Allen, who threw the ball deep to . . . offensive lineman Rich Seubert? But what should have been called pass interference on the Niners was instead called against the Giants for an ineligible man downfield (Seubert). Problem was that Seubert *had* checked in before the play began, and so pass interference should have been called, which the league admitted the following day. Either way, the 49ers won the game, but lost in the next round to the soon-to-be Super Bowl–champion Buccaneers.

24. D—Jacksonville Jaguars. In the last game of Shula's Hall of Fame coaching career, the Dolphins faced the Jags in the divisional round of the playoffs. Hoping to continue his farewell tour, the game instead turned into a disaster, as his team fell behind, 24–0, in the *first quarter*, and would be trounced, 62–7.

25. C—Eric Mangini. The former Patriots assistant (and then Jets head coach), Mangini's information brought controversy to the league and furthered the hatred between the Pats and Jets.

26. D—Ricardo Lockette. With the ball on the 1-yard line and trailing the Pats, 28–24, with 25 seconds left in the game, Seahawks coach Pete Carroll decided to pass the ball instead of run . . . a decision that will forever haunt him.

27. D—Washington Redskins. In the 1940 NFL Championship Game, the Redskins were scorched by the Bears, 73–0.

28. A—Sean McDermott. Intended as a speech to bring his team together during training camp, McDermott quickly apologized to his team and later the media for his poor wording.

29. D—Chicago Bears. The Monsters of the Midway slayed the Cowboys, 44–0, in a game during the 1985 season. Legend has it that Mike Ditka was emotional in the wake of beating his coaching mentor by such a substantial margin.

30. B—Tennessee Titans. In a wild-card-round game, the Pats lost to the Titans, 20–13, in what would be Brady's last game for New England.

31. C—Eleven: Dave Wannstedt (2000–04), Jim Bates* (2004), Nick Saban (2005–06), Cam Cameron (2007), Tony Sparano (2008–11), Todd Bowles* (2011), Joe Philbin (2012–15), Dan Campbell* (2015), Adam Gase (2016–18), Brian Flores (2019–21), Mike McDaniel (2022–present). * Interim head coach.

32. A—Earnest Byner.

33. B—Seattle Seahawks. Up 16–0 at the half, the Seahawks outscored the Packers 22–6 in the second half to send the game to overtime. Receiving the ball in extra time, the Hawks marched down the field, and a 35-yard reception by Jermaine Kearse gave them a 28–22 victory.

34. A—Carson Palmer. After leading the Cardinals to a 13–3 record while throwing 35 TDs to just 11 INTs, Palmer had what may have been the worst game of his career. He would finish the day with four interceptions, three sacks, two fumbles, and a quarterback rating of 43.2.

35. B—Scott Norwood. His kick went wide right to end Buffalo's hopes of winning the Super Bowl. For Bills fans, we'll leave it at that.

36. C–Tony Romo. With 1:19 left on the clock and down 21–20, Martin Gramatica lined up for a 19-yard field goal… only he never got a chance. After receiving the snap, the ball slipped out of Romo's hands as he went to place it down, forcing him to pick it up and scramble for the end zone. He would get brought down by Jordan Babineaux, which essentially ended his team's chances at moving on to the next round.

37. A—1993 Miami Dolphins. While the team started the season strong, they lost their leader, Dan Marino, to a torn Achillies in a game against the Browns. They would win three of their next four with Scott Mitchell at the helm, but then *he* got hurt and would miss the next four games. Steve DeBerg was next up, and he'd help the team win their next two games to go to 9–2, but the magic ran out after that. The Dolphins would drop their final five games of the season to finish 9–7, just missing out on the wild card.

38. A—Minnesota Vikings. During a blizzard that brought around 17 inches of snow in a 48-hour period, the weight of all that snow and ice on the roof of the Hubert H. Humphrey Metrodome gave way, ripping through the roof and covering the field. The disaster would force the team to play their final two home games of the season at Ford Field (home of the Lions) and TCF Bank Stadium, home of the University of Minnesota.

39. D—Stefon Diggs. Down 24–23 with just 10 seconds remaining and on their own 39-yard line, quarterback Case Keenum dropped back and threw a bullet to Diggs by the sideline. If caught, the hope would be that Diggs would be able to get out of bounds, as the Vikings were out of timeouts. But instead of bringing Diggs down, rookie defensive back Marcus Williams instead went for a big hit . . . and missed . . . Diggs was able to turn and run for the end zone and score the game-winning touchdown.

40. B–Whizzinator. Already with two strikes under the league's substance abuse policy, Smith was caught bringing the contraption onto a plane (though said it was "for his cousin"). He was suspended a month later for the rest of the season, and was released by the Vikings before the next year's draft.

41. C—Flipped double-birds to the crowd. Upon coming out of the tunnel before a matchup between the Dolphins and Bills in 1993, Cox shared his displeasure with the Buffalo fans by greeting them with both fingers up . . . which was caught on camera for all to see. The NFL fined him $10,000, and he in turn sued the league on the terms of them protecting players from fan abuse. The league later reduced the fine to $3,000, and Cox dropped the lawsuit.

42. A—Mike Tice. Before beginning is fourth (and final) full season as the head coach of the Vikings, Tice admitted to being a part of the operation, and was fined $100,000 by the league.

43. A—Plaxico Burress. With 35 seconds left in the game, Eli Manning hit Plax for a 12-yard touchdown reception, putting the Giants up, 17–14.

44. B—Rich Gannon. While winning MVP honors for the 2002 season, Gannon's play in the Super Bowl felt more like an LVP. He would throw five interceptions—two of them taken back for touchdowns—one fumble, and five sacks in an unforgettable day for the quarterback.

45. D—Arrested for soliciting a prostitute who turned out to be an undercover cop. He would, surprisingly, still be allowed to play in the Super Bowl. However, most likely due to lack of sleep from being in a jail cell, would give up two key plays that helped the Broncos beat the Falcons, 34–19. It would be his last season in Atlanta.

46. D—Buddy Ryan and Kevin Gilbride. With both coaches sharing barbs during the season, Ryan (the head coach) couldn't hold his contempt for Gilbride (the offensive coordinator) anymore, and after words were exchanged punched the coach in the jaw. Going so far as to say that "Kevin Gilbride will be selling insurance in two years," the two coached together for another season after their altercation.

47. B—1992. Nicknamed "The Comeback" (or "The Choke," depending on who you ask), the Oilers held a 28–3 lead at half-time of an AFC wild-card game. But after a 28-point third quarter (behind four TD passes by Frank Reich, with three of them going to Andre Reed) by the Bills, they were able to send the game to overtime tied at 38. A field goal in overtime gave Buffalo the 41–38 victory.

48. 1: C; 2: A, 3: B, 4: E, 5: D

49. None. Each owner presided over their teams move (Kroenke moving the Rams from St. Louis to Los Angeles, Irsay moving the Colts from Baltimore to Indy, Modell moving the Browns to Baltimore and renaming the franchise as the "Ravens," Mark Davis moving the Raiders from Oakland to Las Vegas.

50. A—Indianapolis Colts. Behind three passing touchdowns by Andrew Luck (four on the day), Indy outscored Kansas City 35–6 in the second half.

51. D—Rod Marinelli. In his third season with the Lions (the previous two finishing 10–22), the 2008 Lions would lose every game of the season. Marinelli would be relieved of his duties at season's end.

52. D—Miami Dolphins. After preseason comments by Broncos coach Sean Payton about Nathaniel Hackett, the team's previous head coach and new offensive coordinator of the Dolphins, Miami put up 726 yards on Denver on their way to a 70–20 shellacking.

53. B—Jackie Smith. The Cowboys ended up settling for a field goal on the drive, and lost the game, 35–31.

54. B—St. Louis Cardinals. Taken sixth overall out of Colorado State, Stouffer would sit out the entire 1987 season, as he and the team were unable to come to a contractual agreement. His rights were later traded to the Seahawks (in exchange for three draft picks). He would go on to play four seasons in the NFL—all with the Seahawks—making 16 starts with a 5–11 record.

55. A—Chicago Bears. Played on December 31, 1988, a dense fog came over Soldier Field in the second quarter, which cut visibility on the field to about 15 to 20 yards. The Bears would prevail over the Eagles, 20–12, but would fall to the 49ers for the conference championship a week later.

56. C—Miami Dolphins. Looking for a new quarterback, Miami was between then-Charger Drew Brees and then-Viking Daunte Culpepper. Concerned over the health of Brees's shoulder after he had torn his labrum the year before, the Dolphins ultimately chose to go with Culpepper, who had missed most of the previous season after damaging three of the four major ligaments in his knee. After just four games, Culpepper had arthroscopic surgery on his previously injured knee, and was done in Miami after just four games (going 1–3). Brees, on the other hand, would play 228 games in NOLA, collecting two AP Offensive Player of the Year Awards, 12 Pro Bowl appearances, and a victory in Super Bowl XLIV (along with being the game's MVP).

57. D—New Orleans Saints. Nicknamed the "Aints," the 1980 Saints went 1–15 on the season, forcing those in attendance to hide their identities with paper bags. Nobody blamed them.

58. B—Roger Craig. With just under six minutes left in regulation, and leading, 13–12, the 49ers looked to run down the clock for the victory. After several runs by Craig, Giants defensive

tackle Erik Howard was able to hit Craig hard enough to jar the ball loose, with Lawrence Taylor recovering the ball. The Giants then drove down the field and kicked a field goal as time expired for the 15–13 victory.

59. C—Dallas Cowboys. Down 28–16 at the start of the fourth quarter, Cowboys quarterback Roger Staubach put his team on his back, throwing for two touchdowns and an amazing comeback over the 49ers. Dallas would win the game, 30–28.

60. A—Vontaze Burfict. After Cincinnati took a 16–15 lead over their division rivals, Ben Roethlisberger was picked off by Burfict with just 1:36 left to go. Hoping to run out the clock, running back Jeremy Hill fumbled the ball on the team's first play of the drive. With the ball on their own 9-yard line, Pittsburgh was able to get the ball to midfield, though they were now out of time outs and had just 21 seconds left on the clock. On the next play, Big Ben went to hit Antonio Brown over the middle, but the ball sailed over his fingers. Problem was that then-thought-to-be hero Vontaze Burfict drilled Brown in the head with his shoulder, garnering a 15-yard personal foul. THAT was followed by *another* personal foul, this time by Adam Jones. That put the ball on the 17-yard line, and Chris Boswell hit a 35-yard field goal to give the Steelers the lead and the win. In just 1:15, Burfict went from the hero to the goat.

Chapter 10

IT'S ALL ABOUT THE BENJAMINS

They say money makes the world go round, and that's especially true in the NFL. An entity that started with annual contracts in the hundreds of dollars, we're now in an era of nine-figure contracts and worldwide endorsement deals. Players and owners alike continue to reap the benefits of an unprecedented sporting windfall. Find out some of the details as to how we got here in this chapter.

1. What Super Bowl had the biggest point spread, and did the winners cover?
   Answer on page 213.

2. True or False: The 2007 Patriots were the only NFL team favored to win 20 games—including the regular season and playoffs—in a single season.
   Answer on page 213.

3. True or False: The 2008 Lions—who finished 0–16—were the underdogs in the greatest point-spread differential in NFL history.
   Answer on page 213.

4. According to the Nevada Gaming Control Board, since they started keeping records on Super Bowl wagering, what two Super Bowls produced losses for Vegas sports books?
   Answer on page 213.

5. Who was the first player to be paid to play the game of football?
   A. Jim Thorpe
   B. Pudge Heffelfinger
   C. Otto Graham
   D. Rocky Brown
   Answer on page 214.

6. In 1892, the Allegheny Athletic Association took a bold step toward modernizing the professional game. What did it do?
   A. Paying referees for their services
   B. Start charging for tickets
   C. Paying multiple players
   D. Build and operate the first known "stadium"
   Answer on page 214.

7. This former Olympian and professional baseball player was inked to a deal with the Canton Bulldogs in 1915 for $250.
   A. Jim Thorpe
   B. Jesse Owens
   C. Sonny Werblin
   D. Cass Davidson
   Answer on page 214.

8. What future Hall of Famer was reportedly the first player to retain an agent who helped negotiate a contract for a 19-game barnstorming tour with the Bears in 1925?
    A. Bronko Nagurski
    B. Ned "Bullet" Byers
    C. Walt Jackson
    D. Red Grange
    Answer on page 214.

9. In 1936, the first overall pick in the inaugural NFL draft, Jay Berwanger, dismayed by the lack of money offered by the Philadelphia Eagles, initially turned down the offer to play professional football. He said he wanted to start a career in what field instead?
    A. Foam-rubber salesman
    B. Broadway actor
    C. Tailor
    D. Fireman
    Answer on page 214.

10. In 1937, Sammy Baugh was the highest-paid player in professional football. Was his salary more or less than $5,000 a season?
    Answer on page 214.

11. In 1956, the NFLPA was formed. Among their demands were a minimum salary structure. What was that number they settled on?
    A. $2,500 a season
    B. $5,000 a season
    C. $1,000 per game
    D. $1,750 per game, plus free haircuts
    Answer on page 214.

12. What quarterback became the highest-paid player in NFL history in 1975, when he signed a two-year deal worth $900,000?
A. Roger Staubach
B. Terry Bradshaw
C. Joe Namath
D. Earl Campbell
Answer on page 214.

13. Before the rookie salary structure was put into place, this quarterback set the standard with a six-year, $78 million deal in 2010, the largest rookie contract in NFL history.
A. Cam Newton
B. Blake Bortles
C. Johnny Manziel
D. Sam Bradford
Answer on page 214–215.

14. Match the football star or coach with their slightly puzzling endorsement deal.
1. Tom Brady   A. Just For Men
2. Jimmy Johnson   B. Skechers
3. Joe Namath   C. Uggs
4. Emmitt Smith   D. Pantyhose
5. Joe Montana   E. Extenze
Answer on page 215.

15. This running back—who also played baseball—shot to fame with a shoe endorsement deal in the late 1980s and early 1990s, where the catchphrase rhymed with his first name. Name the player and the company.
A. Bo Jackson, Nike

B. Brian Bosworth, Adidas
C. Joe Montana, Pony
D. Jerry Rice, Puma
Answer on page 215.

16. What receiver was the first player in the NFL to sign a multi-million–dollar deal with Jordan Brand?
A. Jerry Rice
B. Terry Glenn
C. Terrell Owens
D. Randy Moss
Answer on page 215.

17. Before the 2011 NFL Draft, what soon-to-be-drafted quarterback set a record for wealthiest endorsement deal in league history, at a rate of $1 million annually?
A. Andy Dalton
B. Colin Kaepernick
C. Cam Newton
D. Jake Locker
Answer on page 215.

18. This superstar signed a $35 million deal in 1995, but the team backloaded the salary with so many bonuses in the later years of the contract—ostensibly, to make it cap-friendly—that it caught the eye of the league, which later outlawed such deals in the future.
A. Brett Favre
B. Deion Sanders
C. Terrell Davis
D. John Elway
Answer on page 215.

19. According to ESPN, what is the range for Roger Goodell when it came to his combined salaries for the 2019 and 2020 seasons?
A. Between $15 million and $20 million
B. Between $21 million and $30 million
C. Between $31 million and $40 million
D. More than $40 million
Answer on page 215.

20. True or False: Experienced NFL referees make an average of roughly $12,000 per game.
Answer on page 215.

21. True or False: Referees get paid more for working the Super Bowl.
Answer on page 215.

22. In the most recent round of negotiations between the NFL and TV networks, was the 11-year deal signed worth more or less than $100 billion?
Answer on page 215.

23. True or False: As of 2024, there is an active player who is worth more than a billion dollars.
Answer on page 215.

24. What player was the first to make $50,000 annually for playing football?
A. Bart Starr
B. Johnny Unitas
C. Jim Brown
D. Johnny Lujack
Answer on page 216.

25. What event caused the salaries of some stars to spike in the mid-1960s?
    A. The arrival of the American Football League (AFL).
    B. Players first started hiring agents.
    C. Improvements in equipment led to better statistics.
    D. The creation of the Canadian Football League (CFL).
    Answer on page 216.

26. What player signed a $29 million endorsement deal with Nike in 2017, making him one of the highest-paid endorsers in the league?
    A. Antonio Brown
    B. Johnny Manziel
    C. Tom Brady
    D. Odell Beckham Jr.
    Answer on page 216.

27. This player signed a $2 million endorsement deal with an insurance company, one that allowed him to include his touchdown celebration into the corporate catch phrase.
    A. J. J. Watt
    B. Aaron Rodgers
    C. Ed Reed
    D. Randy Moss
    Answer on page 216.

28. According to *Forbes*, this quarterback made $45 million in endorsements in 2022.
    A. Tom Brady
    B. Peyton Manning
    C. Eli Manning
    D. Dan Marino
    Answer on page 216.

29. The NFL instituted the salary cap in what year?
A. 1985
B. 1988
C. 1994
D. 2000
Answer on page 216.

30. True or False: The initial cap was set at a maximum of $1 million per player.
Answer on page 216.

31. As of 2024, which player had the largest signing bonus in league history?
A. Tom Brady
B. Aaron Rodgers
C. Pat Mahomes
D. Lamar Jackson
Answer on page 216.

32. In March 2021, the league announced a broadcast agreement with a collection of networks that was set to run from 2023 through 2033. Was the final total above or below $100 billion?
Answer on page 216.

33. Before he retired at the end of the 2023 season, what non-quarterback had the highest annual average salary in the NFL?
A. Travis Kelce
B. Aaron Donald
C. Tyreek Hill
D. Saquon Barkley
Answer on page 216.

34. Which owner was hit with the largest fine in NFL history?
A. Jim Irsay
B. Daniel Snyder
C. Robert Kraft
D. Edward DeBartolo Jr.
Answer on page 217.

35. True or False: Ray Rice paid the largest player fine in NFL history.
Answer on page 217.

36. As of 2023, who is the richest owner in the NFL, according to *Forbes*?
A. Jerry Jones
B. Robert Kraft
C. Woody Johnson
D. Rob Walton
Answer on page 217.

37. True or False: Usher received $1.5 million for performing during halftime of Super Bowl LVIII?
Answer on page 217.

38. What was the financial range when it comes to the bonus each player on the Chiefs received for winning Super Bowl LVIII?
A. Between $100,000 and $199,999
B. Between $200,000 and $299,999
C. Between $300,000 and $399,999
D. More than $400,000
Answer on page 217.

39. Which player, after he was released in 2024, provided the biggest "dead cap hit" of all time against his old team?
A. Russell Wilson, $85 million
B. Matt Ryan, $41 million
C. Tom Brady, $35 million
D. Carson Wentz, $34 million
Answer on page 217.

40. As of 2023–24, what is the minimum salary for NFL players with one year of experience?
A. $150,000
B. $550,000
C. $650,000
D. $750,000
Answer on page 217.

41. As of 2023, these were the top five free-agent deals signed, ranked by average annual value (AAV).Fill in the blanks:
1. _____, Minnesota Vikings, 2023: Three years, $84M ($28M AAV).
T-2. _____ Tampa Bay Buccaneers, 2020: Two years, $50M ($25M AAV).
T-2. _____, Indianapolis Colts, 2020: One year, $25M.
4. _____, San Francisco 49ers, 2021: Six years, $138M ($23M AAV).
5. _____, Jacksonville Jaguars, 2019: Four years, $88M ($22M AAV).
Answer on page 217.

42. Who was the first player in NFL history to sign a contract worth $1 million?
   A. Fran Tarkenton
   B. Johnny Unitas
   C. Johnny "Lam" Jones
   D. Vince Ferragamo
   Answer on page 218.

43. How much—in base salary—did Tom Brady earn over the course of his playing career?
   A. Between $150 million and $200 million
   B. Between $201 million and $250 million
   C. Between $251 million and $300 million
   D. Over $300 million
   Answer on page 218.

44. True or False: Lawrence Taylor was the first high-profile free agent to change teams?
   Answer on page 218.

45. True or false: As of 2024, the Giants are the most valuable franchise in the NFL
   Answer on page 218.

46. As of 2023, what is the least valuable NFL franchise?
   A. Green Bay Packers
   B. Cincinnati Bengals
   C. New York Jets
   D. Detroit Lions
   Answer on page 218.

47. What was the most expensive stadium to build?
   A. SoFi Stadium, Los Angeles
   B. MetLife Stadium, New Jersey
   C. Mercedes-Benz Stadium, Atlanta
   D. Allegiant Stadium, Las Vegas
   Answer on page 218.

Chapter 10

IT'S ALL ABOUT THE BENJAMINS

ANSWERS

1. The largest spread in Super Bowl history was for Super Bowl XXIX. The Niners were an 18.5-point favorite against the Chargers, and San Francisco easily covered the spread, winning, 49–26.

2. False. The 2021 Chiefs were the only team in league history to be favored in 20 games in a season, including the playoffs. They would end up falling short of that number, going 12–5 on the season and winning two playoff games (falling to the Bengals in the conference championship game).

3. False. In a 2013 game between the 0–5 Jaguars and 5–0 Broncos, multiple sports books had Jacksonville as anywhere between a 26.5- to 28-point favorite. That's believed to be the largest spread in league history. The Broncos would win the game, 35–19, but fall below the spread.

4. According to reports, sports books lost $2.57 million on Super Bowl XLII, when the Giants upended the then-undefeated Patriots, and almost $397,000 in the wake of Super Bowl XXIX, when the Niners blew out the Chargers.

5. B—Pudge Heffelfinger. Considered the first athlete to play American football professionally, the Pro Football Hall of Fame unearthed a document which indicated that Heffelfinger received $500 in cash to play in a game on November 12, 1892.

6. C—Paying multiple players. With Heffelfinger being the first, the Allegheny Athletic Association signed multiple players in 1892 and 1893, sparking the birth of the pro game.

7. A—Jim Thorpe. A two-time gold medalist, Thorpe would play six seasons in professional baseball and eight in professional football, as well as playing basketball for the World Famous Indians, a traveling basketball team from Ohio, and even considering going pro in hockey for the Tecumseh Hockey Club of Toronto.

8. D—Red Grange, who retained theater owner C. C. Pyle as his agent, with the two reportedly making $150,000 on the deal.

9. A—Foam rubber salesman. Berwanger allegedly turned down the $125–$150 per game that was offered, and never heard an answer to his request for $25,000 for two seasons.

10. More. According to *Forbes*, Baugh's $8,000 annual salary was the highest in professional football that year.

11. B—$5,000 a season. The players asked for $5,000 per season (around $57,000 today), plus $50 for each preseason game.

12. C—Joe Namath. The Jets' quarterback was a hot commodity among several football leagues, including the WFL, which made financial overtures to him prior to the 1975 season.

13. D—Sam Bradford. Taken first overall in the 2010 draft by the Rams, Bradford would spend just four years in St. Louis, compiling a 18–30–1 record. He would be out of the league by 2018.

14. 1:C, 2:E, 3:D, 4:A, 5:B

15. A—Bo Jackson, who was the star of Nike's "Bo Knows" campaign.

16. D—Randy Moss. In 2000, Nike came out with the "Jordan Super Freak," a nod to Moss and his talents.

17. C—Cam Newton. His mega-contract with Under Armour consisted of both a shoe and apparel deal.

18. B—Deion Sanders. His salary in the first year of the deal provided him with a base salary of just $178,000. The deal was one of several in the mid-1990s that led the league to start cracking down on teams looking to circumvent the salary cap.

19. D—More than $40 million. According to ESPN, Goodell earned $63.9 million in combined salary between the two seasons.

20. True. While that amount varies when it comes to overall experience—rookie referees have been known to make roughly $1,000 per game—the high end of the scale will routinely see referees make five figures.

21. True. According to multiple reports, referees get an additional $30,000 to $50,000 for working the Super Bowl, depending on their level of experience.

22. More. It was for $110 billion.

23. False. While several active players have accumulated more than a quarter-billion in career earnings, no active player is currently worth more than a billion dollars.

24. C—Jim Brown. The Browns running back was making $50,000 annually in 1964, making him the highest-paid player in the league.

25. A—The arrival of the American Football League (AFL). The new league threatened to draw players from the NFL—and did so in several instances. As a result, players had more leverage when it came to contract negotiations.

26. D—Odell Beckham Jr. OBJ's five-year deal with Nike was one of several endorsements for the receiver, including ones with EA Sports, Foot Locker, and others.

27. B—Aaron Rodgers. Endorsing State Farm Insurance, the Packers quarterback worked his "Discount Double Check" touchdown celebration into the company's commercials and lexicon.

28. A—Tom Brady. Per *Forbes*, Brady also made $31 million in endorsements in 2021, coming through connections with companies such as Aston Martin, Under Armour, and Hertz.

29. C—1994. After it was determined in 1992 that the NFL had violated antitrust rules by refusing to grant players the opportunity to become free agents, the first salary cap was introduced in 1994.

30. False. Each team's salary cap was set at $34.6 million.

31. D—Lamar Jackson. His newly signed contract is worth $260 million, with a signing bonus of $72.5 million.

32. Above. The deal was reportedly worth just over $110 billion, or $10 billion annually.

33. B—Aaron Donald. A 10-time Pro Bowler, 8-time All-Pro, and 3-time DPOY had an annual average salary of $31.6 million.

34. B—Daniel Snyder. The former owner of the Washington Commanders, Snyder was fined $60 million as part of an investigation into financial misconduct in 2023, with the league forcing him to sell the franchise shortly after the verdict.

35. False. Quarterback Deshaun Watson was fined $5 million for violating the league's personal conduct policy in 2022.

36. D—Rob Walton. The head of the ownership group at the controls of the Denver Broncos, the heir to the Walmart franchise (according to *Forbes*) is worth $59 billion.

37. False. Halftime performers are not paid for their performances.

38. C—Between 300,000 and $399,999. According to the NFL Players Association collective bargaining agreement, players on the winning team earned $338,000 in bonus pay.

39. A—Russell Wilson, $85 million. After signing a five-year contract extension with the Broncos worth $242.6 million, Wilson would go on to have two subpar seasons in Denver, going 11–19. Releasing him after his second season, the Broncos took a dead cap hit of $85 million so that the quarterback could play elsewhere (signing with the Steelers four days after his release).

40. D—$750,000. For the 2024 season, the rookie minimum salary will increase to $795,000.

41. 1: Kirk Cousins, Minnesota Vikings, 2023 (three years, $84M—$28M AAV); T-2: Tom Brady, Tampa Bay Buccaneers, 2020 (two years, $50M—$25M AAV); T-2: Philip Rivers, Indianapolis Colts, 2020 (one year, $25M); 4: Trent Williams, San Francisco 49ers, 2021 (six years, $138M—$23M AAV); 5: Nick Foles, Jacksonville Jaguars, 2019 (four years, $88M—$22M AAV)

42. C—Johnny "Lam" Jones, who signed a six-year, $2.1 million deal with the Jets in 1980.

43. D—Over $300 million. He is estimated to have earned around $450 million over his 23-year playing career.

44. False. After eight seasons as a member of the Eagles, Reggie White signed a four-year deal worth $17 million in 1993 to join the Packers. Lawrence Taylor would spend his entire 13-year career with the Giants.

45. False: According to *Forbes*, the Cowboys are the most valuable franchise in the NFL, estimated at $9 billion.

46. B—Cincinnati Bengals. Of the thirty-two NFL teams, the Bengals are last in value, estimated at $4 billion.

47. A—SoFi Stadium, Los Angeles. Home to the Rams and Chargers, SoFi cost a reported $4.9 billion to construct (which is more than double the second-most expensive, Allegiant Stadium in Las Vegas, which cost $1.9 billion).

Chapter 11

MAGIC MOMENTS

If you're a Bears fan, you know where you were when Devin Hester took the opening kickoff to the house to open Super Bowl XLI with a bang. If you're a Colts fan, you know just how important Marlin Jackson was to the history of the franchise. And if you're a Cowboys supporter, Emmitt Smith's gutsy performance at the end of the 1993 season against the Giants remains seared into your memory. This chapter looks at some of the most memorable moments in NFL history, with a focus on the individuals at the center of those epic achievements.

1. What town did the first-ever team to win the professional football championship come from?
   A. Chicago
   B. Louisville
   C. Akron
   D. Buffalo
   Answer on page 237.

2. In one of the greatest individual performances in NFL history, this player scored every point for the Chicago Cardinals in a 40–6 win over the Bears in 1929.
   A. Red Grange
   B. Bronko Nagurski
   C. Ernie Nevers
   D. Jim Thorpe
   Answer on page 237.

3. Don Hutson did many great things over the course of his career, but what did he accomplish in 1945 that made him a Packers Packers legend?
   A. Finish a game with three sacks and three touchdowns.
   B. Score 29 points in one quarter.
   C. Led the Packers defense with 10 interceptions.
   D. Was the first player/coach in Packers history.
   Answer on page 237.

4. What Rams quarterback set the franchise record for most passing yards in one game in a September 28, 1951, clash against the New York Yanks?
   A. Norm Van Brocklin
   B. Bobby Layne
   C. Slingin' Sammy Baugh
   D. Rushton McGraw
   Answer on page 237.

5. This running back holds the NFL mark for rushing yards in a game with 296.
   A. Walter Payton
   B. Jim Brown

C. Derrick Henry
D. Adrian Peterson
Answer on page 237.

6. What rookie running back averaged a whopping 24 yards per touch (on 14 touches, including work as a returner) during a 1965 contest?
A. Jim Brown
B. Charley Taylor
C. Ken Willard
D. Gale Sayers
Answer on page 238.

7. In the final week of the 1993 regular season, Emmitt Smith suffered a separated shoulder but still managed to finish with 229 total yards and a touchdown. Who was Dallas' opponent?
A. San Francisco 49ers
B. Philadelphia Eagles
C. Washington Redskins
D. New York Giants
Answer on page 238.

8. For all of the greatness he showed as a member of the Rams, the best single-game performance of Kurt Warner's career came as a member of what franchise?
A. New York Giants
B. Arizona Cardinals
C. San Diego Chargers
D. New England Patriots
Answer on page 238.

9. Guy Chamberlin was the coach of the team that won the first back-to-back NFL titles in league history, in 1922 and 1923. What team did he lead?
   A. Akron Pros
   B. Milwaukee Badgers
   C. Canton Bulldogs
   D. Pittsburgh Pirates
   Answer on page 238.

10. Who was the coach of the Packers team that was the first NFL franchise to win three consecutive league titles—1929, 1930, and 1931?
    A. Richard Evans
    B. Vince Lombardi
    C. Bart Starr
    D. Curly Lambeau
    Answer on page 238.

11. What is George "Wildcat" Wilson's claim to fame?
    A. The star of the 1928 Providence Steamrollers, which won the NFL title.
    B. The first player to spike a football.
    C. He popularized the forward pass.
    D. Created the "wildcat" offense.
    Answer on page 238.

12. Stanford Jennings is known for what memorable moment in Cincinnati Bengals' history?
    A. He scored the game-winning touchdown in the AFC title game that lifted the Bengals into Super Bowl XXIII.
    B. He ran back a kickoff against the Niners in Super Bowl XXIII.

C. His ill-timed fumble paved the way for a Cincinnati playoff loss.

D. He sacked Ben Roethlisberger to seal a Cincinnati playoff win.

Answer on page 238.

13. On the 2020 play that came to be known as the "Hail Murray," Arizona quarterback Kyler Murray hit what wide receiver with the game-winning touchdown pass to beat the Bills?

A. DeAndre Hopkins

B. Larry Fitzgerald

C. Andy Isabella

D. Christian Kirk

Answer on page 239.

14. What Patriots wide receiver tossed a touchdown pass to help spark a New England comeback against the Ravens in a divisional playoff game in the 2014 postseason?

A. Danny Amendola

B. Julian Edelman

C. Chris Hogan

D. Brandon LaFell

Answer on page 239.

15. Jim Brown rushed for 114 yards in Cleveland's 27–0 win over the Colts in the 1964 NFL Championship Game. Who else helped power the Browns' offense that afternoon?

A. Otto Graham

B. Chubbs Peterson

C. Gary Collins

D. Art Blakey

Answer on page 239.

16. J. J. Watt provided a boost in the Texans' first-ever playoff game with an unexpected touchdown. What did he do?
    A. A scoop-and-score for a touchdown off a fumble.
    B. He lined up at tight end and caught a pass.
    C. He returned a kick for a score.
    D. A pick six.
    Answer on page 239.

17. What did Steve Gleason do in the 2006 regular-season opener that jump-started the Saints' memorable post-Katrina run?
    A. Threw three touchdown passes
    B. Kicked the game-winning field goal.
    C. Caught and ran for a touchdown.
    D. Blocked a punt.
    Answer on page 239.

18. Which Colts defender intercepted Tom Brady at the end of the 2006 AFC Championship Game to send Indianapolis to the Super Bowl?
    A. Dwight Freeney
    B. Bob Sanders
    C. Marlin Jackson
    D. Kenny Moore II
    Answer on page 239.

19. What Jets running back rushed for a game-high 121 yards to help New York upset the Colts in Super Bowl III?
    A. Emerson Boozer
    B. Tom Matte
    C. Matt Snell
    D. Darren Daye
    Answer on page 239–240.

20. This Tampa Bay defensive back sparked the Bucs to Super Bowl XXXVII with a dramatic pick six in the NFC Championship Game?
A. Darrelle Revis
B. Ronde Barber
C. Tiki Barber
D. Antoine Winfield
Answer on page 240.

21. What Carolina receiver hauled in a 69-yard touchdown catch in double overtime of a 2003 playoff game against the Rams to carry the Panthers to the win.
A. Muhsin Muhammad
B. Ricky Proehl
C. Torry Holt
D. Steve Smith Sr.
Answer on page 240.

22. True or False: Former Steelers running back Willie Parker holds the NFL playoff record for longest run from scrimmage.
Answer on page 240.

23. While the David Tyree catch in Super Bowl XLII against the Patriots was one of the most memorable moments in Super Bowl history, an Eli Manning pass to another New York pass catcher in the Super Bowl four years later was almost as dramatic. Who was the receiver, and name the opponent.
A. Mario Manningham vs. the New England Patriots
B. Jeremy Shockey vs. the New England Patriots
C. Brandon Jacobs vs. the Pittsburgh Steelers
D. Phil McConkey vs. the Denver Broncos
Answer on page 240.

24. True or False: Denver's Tim Tebow's dramatic touchdown pass in an overtime playoff win in early 2012 went to Demaryius Thomas.
Answer on page 240.

25. True or False: Adam Vinatieri's kick that gave the Patriots a lead late in the fourth quarter of Super Bowl XXXVIII was the last play of the game.
Answer on page 240.

26. Name the three players who touched the ball—and the correct order they handled it—on the memorable "Philly Special" play in Super Bowl LII.
Answer on page 240–241.

27. Who were the two Miami receivers involved in the famous "hook and ladder" play that was executed to perfection in the 1981 playoffs against San Diego?
A. Mark Clayton and Mark Duper
B. Jimmy Cefalo and Norris Weese
C. Duriel Harris and Tony Nathan
D. Bhavan Suri and Dan Brem
Answer on page 241.

28. What did San Diego tight end Kellen Winslow NOT do in that same game, an overtime win for the Chargers?
A. Block a Miami field-goal attempt.
B. Catch a touchdown pass.
C. Finish with more than 100 receiving yards.
D. Run for a touchdown.
Answer on page 241.

29. Which member of the Titans initially received the kickoff that started the Music City Miracle?
A. Lorenzo Neal
B. Frank Wycheck
C. Kevin Dyson
D. Eddie George
Answer on page 241.

30. Who was the intended receiver on the play that ended up with the ball in the hands of Franco Harris and the Steelers celebrating the "Immaculate Reception?"
A. Lynn Swann
B. Frenchy Fuqua
C. John Stallworth
D. Rocky Bleier
Answer on page 241.

31. True or False: "Red Right 88" was a successful play call that led to a postseason win.
Answer on page 241.

32. In 2022, the Las Vegas Lateral involved two players with the same last name. What were their names?
A. Jones
B. Johnson
C. Smith
D. Webster
Answer on page 241.

33. In December 2010, the Eagles put the capper on a comeback win over the Giants when a punt returner took it back 65 yards for the walk-off score … after initially fumbling the ball when he first received the punt. Who was the returner?
A. Boston Scott
B. Freddie Mitchell
C. DeSean Jackson
D. Darren Sproles
Answer on page 241.

34. On the Eagles' memorable 4th-and-26 play that took place during a divisional contest against the Packers, who was the quarterback and who caught the pass?
A. Ron Jaworski and Mike Quick
B. Jalen Hurts and DK Metcalf
C. Nick Foles and Corey Clement
D. Donovan McNabb and Freddie Mitchell
Answer on page 242.

35. True or False: "The Miracle in Motown" was a pass from Detroit's Dan Orlovsky to Calvin Johnson to beat the Packers in a dramatic 2006 victory.
Answer on page 242.

36. Who was the New Orleans defender who intercepted Minnesota's Brett Favre in the waning moments of regulation during the 2009 NFC Championship Game?
A. Jonathan Vilma
B. Tracy Porter
C. Darren Sharper
D. Malcolm Jenkins
Answer on page 242.

37. Which Steelers receiver caught what turned out to be the game-winning touchdown in the Super Bowl XLIII win over the Cardinals?
A. Nate Washington
B. Hines Ward
C. Heath Miller
D. Santonio Holmes
Answer on page 242.

38. Who was the Baltimore receiver who hauled in the pass known as the "Mile High Miracle" during a 2012 AFC divisional playoff game in Denver?
A. Steve Smith Sr.
B. Derrick Mason
C. Jacoby Jones
D. Jason Peppers
Answer on page 242.

39. The receiver who ended up catching the pass in a 1980 game—a play that was dubbed "The Miracle at the Met"—ended up going on to a second career as a sportscaster. Who was he?
A. Jimmy Cefalo
B. Bob Trumpy
C. Ahmad Rashad
D. Cris Collinsworth
Answer on page 242.

40. Who scored the touchdown for the Dolphins to beat the Patriots that helped complete the "Miami Miracle" in December 2018?
A. Jaylen Waddle
B. Kenyan Drake
C. Brian Hartline
D. Josh Gordon
Answer on page 243.

41. Who is credited with throwing the first "Hail Mary" touchdown pass?
A. Terry Bradshaw
B. Fran Tarkenton
C. Steve Grogan
D. Roger Staubach
Answer on page 243.

42. Who is credited with catching the first "Hail Mary" touchdown pass?
A. Lynn Swann
B. Drew Pearson
C. Stanley Morgan
D. Ahmad Rashad
Answer on page 243.

43. A classic 1974 AFC divisional playoff game produced a late moment that was later referred to as the "Sea of Hands." What two teams were involved in that contest?
A. Kansas City Chiefs and New York Jets
B. Pittsburgh Steelers and New England Patriots
C. Miami Dolphins and Oakland Raiders
D. Baltimore Colts and San Diego Chargers
Answer on page 243.

44. True or False: "The Catch"—the memorable pass play that went from Joe Montana to Dwight Clark in the 1981 postseason—took place in the NFC divisional round.
Answer on page 243.

45. True or False: Marshawn Lynch's legendary "Beast Mode" run against the Saints went for more than 50 yards.
Answer on page 243.

46. Who was the Green Bay offensive lineman who delivered the key block to spring Bart Starr for a late touchdown in the famed "Ice Bowl" contest between the Packers and Cowboys?
A. Jerry Kramer
B. Bob Skoronski
C. Ken Bowman
D. Forrest Gregg
Answer on page 243.

47. Which Kansas City receiver hauled in the game-winning touchdown pass from Patrick Mahomes in overtime of Super Bowl LVIII?
A. Travis Kelce
B. Rashee Rice
C. Mecole Hardman
D. Marquez Valdes-Scantling
Answer on page 243–244.

48. What Jacksonville kicker delivered a dramatic walk-off win in an AFC wild-card contest against the Chargers during the 2022 playoffs?
A. Josh Scobee
B. Riley Patterson
C. Chad Ryland
D. Harris Butker
Answer on page 244.

49. True or False: Randy Moss holds the NFL record for most receiving yards in a playoff game, set during the 2007 divisional playoff against the Jaguars.
Answer on page 244.

50. What Philadelphia linebacker made a key stop late in the 1960 NFL Championship Game between the Eagles and Packers, keeping Green Bay's Jim Taylor out of the end zone and securing Vince Lombardi's only playoff defeat?
A. Bill Bergey
B. Chuck Weber
C. Maxie Baughan
D. Chuck Bednarik
Answer on page 244.

51. Which New York Giants defender delivered a key hit on San Francisco quarterback Joe Montana to force a key fumble late in the 1990 NFC Championship Game?
A. Lawrence Taylor
B. Leonard Marshall
C. Carl Banks
D. Pepper Johnson
Answer on page 244.

52. What Denver quarterback was at the controls of "The Drive" in a 1987 playoff win against the Browns?
A. John Elway
B. Craig Morton
C. Gary Kubiak
D. Tommy Maddox
Answer on page 244.

53. Who was under center in 2020, when the Browns won their first postseason game since 2002 over the Steelers?
A. Case Keenum
B. Johnny Manziel
C. Jacoby Brissett
D. Baker Mayfield
Answer on page 244.

54. What Bengals quarterback delivered the first road playoff win in franchise history, despite being the most-sacked quarterback to win a postseason game?
A. Boomer Esiason
B. Akili Smith
C. Ken Anderson
D. Joe Burrow
Answer on page 244.

55. This Miami kicker ended the longest playoff game in NFL history with a 37-yard field goal.
A. Olindo Mare
B. John Smith
C. Garo Yepremian
D. Raul Allegre
Answer on page 245.

56. What Patriots defensive back picked off Peyton Manning three times in the 2003 AFC Championship Game?
A. Tyrone Poole
B. Rodney Harrison
C. Ty Law
D. Otis Smith
Answer on page 245.

57. A fake spike—followed by a touchdown pass that was the difference—helped deliver a 1994 win on the road. Who was the quarterback who managed to pull off the trickery?
A. Dan Marino
B. Steve DeBerg
C. Drew Bledsoe
D. Duke Silver
Answer on page 245.

58. Which quarterback had the most passing yards in a game in which he had a perfect passer rating?
A. Ken O'Brien
B. Aaron Rodgers
C. Jared Goff
D. Deshaun Watson
Answer on page 245.

59. As of 2023, there have been 122 instances of a perfect QB rating when passing for at least 100 yards. Of those, how many ended in a loss?
A. 0
B. 9
C. 17

D. 34
Answer on page 245.

60. As of 2023, who are the five quarterbacks to have more than one game with a perfect passer rating?
Answer on page 245.

Chapter 11

MAGIC MOMENTS

ANSWERS

1. C—Akron. The 1920 Akron Pros, led by Fritz Pollard—the first African American coach—gave up seven points all season and shut out their opponents in 10 of 11 games.

2. C—Ernie Nevers, who scored six touchdowns and added four extra points in the Cardinals' shellacking of the Bears.

3. B—Score 29 points in one quarter all by himself. In a game against the Lions, Hutson threw four touchdown passes in the second quarter, along with five extra points, to help lead the Pack to victory, 57–21.

4. A—Norm Van Brocklin. In the first game of the 1951 season, Van Brocklin passed for 554 yards and five touchdowns in a 54–14 victory over the Yanks. Fun fact: the two players next on the list are Warren Moon (1990) and Matt Schaub (2012), who threw for 527 yards (with Schaub's game going into overtime).

5. Adrian Peterson. "All Day" ran for 296 yards and three touchdowns in a game against the Chargers, on November 4, 2007 (his rookie year!). One yard behind him on the all-time list is Jamal Lewis, who rushed for 295 yards in 2003.

6. D—Gale Sayers. In a win over San Francisco (61–20), Sayers finished with 336 total yards, which included six total touchdowns (an 80-yard passing touchdown, four rushing touchdowns, and an 85-yard punt return to the house), which is tied for the most all-time.

7. D—New York Giants. Smith led the Cowboys to a win that clinched the NFL East and home-field advantage through the playoffs, on the way to the second of back-to-back titles for Dallas (and a league MVP Award).

8. B—Arizona Cardinals. In the opening round of the 2009 playoffs against the Packers, Warner had more touchdowns than incompletions, going 29-for-33 for 379 yards and five touchdowns in the team's 51–45 victory.

9. C—Canton Bulldogs. Coach Chamberlin's teams went a combined 21–0–3 in those two seasons. Also the team's running back, he rushed for seven TDs in 1922.

10. D—Curly Lambeau. Going a combined 34–5–2, Lambeau led the Pack to their first championships since their inception in 1921 (as a member of the American Professional Football Association, AFPA).

11. A—The star of the 1928 Providence Steam Roller, which won the NFL title—the first team from New England to win the NFL Championship.

12. B—He ran back a kickoff against the Niners in Super Bowl XXIII. The team's lone touchdown of the game, Jenning's 93-yard kickoff return in the third quarter game the Bengals a 13–6 lead, but the team would fall to the 49ers behind Joe Montana's famous, game-winning drive.

13. A—DeAndre Hopkins. With just 11 seconds left on the clock, Murray launched a 43-yard pass into the air, which was brought down by Hopkins to give the Cardinals a 32–30 victory over the Bills.

14. B—Julian Edelman. Down a touchdown in the third quarter, Edelman, who played quarterback at Kent State, received a lateral from Tom Brady and hit a striding Danny Amendola for a 51-yard touchdown. The score would tie the game, and the Pats would go on to win, 35–31.

15. C—Gary Collins. While Brown led the team on the ground, Collins collected 130 receiving yards and was the only player to get in the end zone for Cleveland, scoring three touchdowns.

16. D—A pick six. With the game tied at 10, Watt intercepted Andy Dalton and took the ball 29 yards to the end zone, giving the Texans a 17–10 lead. They would score two additional touchdowns for a 31–10 victory, the first playoff win in franchise history.

17. D—Blocked a punt. In the team's first home game since Hurricane Katrina, Steve Gleason blocked a punt on the Falcons' first drive, which was recovered by Curtis DeLoatch for a touchdown.

18. C—Marlin Jackson. Nicknamed "Manning's Revenge," the Patriots were driving down the field with 24 seconds left and trailing, 38–34. Known for his late-game heroics, Brady's next pass—intended for tight end Ben Watson—was picked off by Jackson to seal the team's victory and a ticket to the Super Bowl.

19. A game known more for Joe Naimath's guarantee, Snell carried the team on his back. With 30 carries for 121 yards, he scored the Jets' only touchdown on the day, helping them win the franchise's first Super Bowl, 16–7.

20. B—Ronde Barber, whose 92-yard pick six gave the Bucs a 27–10 lead, sealing their victory and ticket to the Super Bowl.

21. D—Steve Smith Sr. Up by 11 with a little over two minutes left in regulation, the Rams scored a touchdown and a regulation-ending field goal to send the game into overtime. With the ball to start the second OT (and on 3rd-and-13, as it was a continuation of the first OT), Jake Delhomme hit Smith down the middle, where he sped past defenders for a 69-yard game-ending touchdown. He would finish with 163 receiving yards on the day.

22. False. That record is held by Jaguar Fred Taylor, who set the mark with a 90-yard run from scrimmage in a 1999 postseason game against the Dolphins.

23. A—Mario Manningham against the Patriots. Down by two with just under four minutes left in regulation, Eli Manning hit a streaking Manningham for a 38-yard reception that was so close to being out of bounds that the Patriots challenged the call. New York would get in the end zone at the end of the drive, and with just under a minute left held Brady and the Pats in check for their second Super Bowl victory over New England.

24. True. Tebow's 80-yard touchdown pass to Thomas at the start of overtime led Denver to a 29–23 win over the Steelers.

25. False. There were four seconds left on the clock, but Patriots linebacker Matt Chatham tackled Carolina's Rod Smith on the ensuing kickoff, ending the game.

26. The ball was snapped to running back Corey Clement, who ran left and flipped it to tight end Trey Burton. Burton tossed the ball to quarterback Nick Foles, who ran a route to the right corner of the end zone for the score.

27. With six seconds left in the first half and the ball on the Chargers 41-yard line, Harris caught a pass from quarterback Don Stock, and flipped the ball to Nathan who ran it in for the score.

28. D—Run for a touchdown. Winslow had 13 receptions for 166 yards and a touchdown, along with blocking a potential game-winning field goal at the end of regulation, which sent the game into overtime.

29. A—Lorenzo Neal. Down 16–15 with just 16 seconds left in regulation, Buffalo sent a high kick that was caught by the fullback Neal, who immediately handed the ball off to Wycheck. Wycheck then threw a "backwards throw" to Dyson, who took the ball 75 yards for the memorable score.

30. B—Frenchy Fuqua. While the pass was meant for Fuqua, the ball pinballed away after a big hit from Jack Tatum, landing in the hands of Harris who took it the distance for the score.

31. False: "Red Right 88" was the play call from the Browns at the end of a postseason game in 1981 that saw Oakland safety Mike Davis pick off quarterback Brian Sipe in the end zone to finish the game.

32. A—Jones. Patriots quarterback Mac Jones threw the initial ball, and Chandler Jones of the Raiders ultimately picked it off and ran it back for the game-winning score.

33. C—DeSean Jackson. Taking the ball to the house as time expired, Jackson helped the Eagles beat the Giants, 38–31.

34. D—Donovan McNabb and Freddie Mitchell. Down three with 1:12 left to go, and on 4th-and-26, McNabb hit Michell for 28 yards and the first down. The Eagles were able to send the game into overtime after a David Akers field goal as time expired. Akers would come up big again, hitting the game-winning field goal in overtime to give Philly the win.

35. False. With no time on the clock and on their own 39-yard line, Green Bay's Aaron Rodgers scrambled out of the pocket and delivered a Hail Mary pass that found Richard Rodgers in the end zone to beat the Lions.

36. B—Tracy Porter. Nicknamed "The Snafu in the Superdome," with just 18 seconds left in regulation in a tie game, and the Vikings close to field goal range, Favre threw a pass across his body that was intercepted by Porter, sending the game into overtime. The Saints would go on to win the game, sending them into the Super Bowl, which they would win two weeks later.

37. D—Santonio Holmes. With under a minute to go and the Steelers down three, Roethlisberger found Holmes in the back of the end zone, where he pulled in the catch and tip-toed inbounds, giving Pittsburgh the lead and a Super Bowl victory.

38. C—Jacoby Jones. Slipping behind the Denver defense, Jones hauled in the Hail Mary from Joe Flacco for the score that set the stage for a Baltimore victory.

39. C—Ahmad Rashad. After catching the ball, Rashad lateraled the ball to Ted Brown, who ran for extra yards and then out of bounds, stopping the clock. The play would help the Vikings complete an impressive late-season comeback against the Browns.

40. B—Kenyan Drake. Needing to go 70 yards in six seconds, the Dolphins hoped that a gadget play would help them get into the end zone. The play went as follows: Ryan Tannehill passes it to Kenny Stills, who laterals it to DaVante Parker, who laterals it to Kenyon Drake who, after showing lateral, ran toward paydirt. With one man to beat, Pats tight end Rob Gronkowski, Drake ran past him for the touchdown and miraculous victory.

41. D—Roger Staubach. The Cowboys gunslinger tossed a late game-winner to pull off an upset victory over the Vikings in a 1975 NFC playoff game. After the game, Staubach said that he heaved the ball downfield, and then closed his eyes and "said a Hail Mary." The term stuck.

42. B—Drew Pearson, Staubach's all-time favorite target, pulled in the 50-yard Hail Mary. He would end up catching 40 touchdowns from Staubach in his career.

43. C—Dolphins and Raiders. Miami faced Oakland, and the Raiders ended up winning when quarterback Ken Stabler tossed the game-winning touchdown pass to Clarence Davis, who wrested the ball away from multiple defenders for the score.

44. False. It was in the 1981 NFC Championship Game.

45. True. Lynch's run broke a number of tackles (eight by my count), going 79 yards to paydirt.

46. A—Jerry Kramer, who delivered a "wedge block" on Dallas defensive lineman Jethro Pugh to clear a path for Starr's touchdown.

47. C—Mecole Hardman. After spending the first four years of his career in Kansas City, Hardman signed as a free agent with the Jets. After five games with just one reception, he was traded *back* to the Chiefs. This obviously worked out for KC, as

Hardman pulled in three receptions for 57 yards, including the game-winner.

48. B—Riley Patterson. Down by 20 at the half, Jacksonville outscored the Chargers 24–3 the rest of the way, with Patterson's 36-yard field goal sealing the incredible comeback.

49. False. The mark is held by Buffalo's Eric Moulds, who had 240 yards on nine catches in a 1998 AFC wild-card game against Miami (though his team wound up losing, 24–17).

50. D—Chuck Bednarik, who made the play and held Taylor down until the clock ticked down to zero.

51. B—Leonard Marshall. The hit, which also knocked Montana out of the game, set up the Giants for a 15–13 victory on the way to their second Super Bowl victory in five years.

52. A—John Elway. Starting on their own 2-yard line, Elway marched the Broncos down the length of the field and into the end zone and sending the game into overtime. A field goal by Rich Karlis in OT would seal the game for Denver, as Elway finished the day with 244 passing yards.

53. D—Baker Mayfield. After a dozen losing seasons and almost twenty since making the playoffs, Mayfield finished his first-career playoff game by going 21-for-34 for 263 yards and three touchdowns. The victory was also Cleveland's first road win over the Steelers since 2003, and first road playoff win since 1969.

54. D—Joe Burrow. Taken down nine times in the game, Burrow kept his composure and threw for 347 yards, leading Cincinnati to a 19–16 win over Tennessee in the 2021 AFC divisional round.

55. C—Garo Yepremian. With the game tied at 24 in the 1971 AFC divisional round between the Dolphins and Chiefs, nobody was able to get on the board in the first overtime. Then, 7:40 into the second overtime, Miami's Yepremian hit a 37-yard field goal to give his team the win over Kansas City. While the Dolphins would lose to the Cowboys in Super Bowl VI, they would win the next two.

56. C—Ty Law. The Hall of Fame defensive back's performance in the game played a sizeable role in the Patriots beating Manning and the Colts, 24–14. They'd continue their success in the Super Bowl, where they'd prevail over the Panthers for their second SB victory in three years.

57. A—Dan Marino. After completing a pass to Ingram that put the ball on the 8-yard line with 37 seconds left in regulation, Marino got his team to the line, motioning that he was to spike the ball and stop the clock. Instead, he caught the Jets defense unaware and hit Ingram in the end zone for the touchdown and the comeback victory.

58. C—Jared Goff. Passing for 465 yards and five touchdowns while completing 26-of-33 passes, Goff led the Rams to a 38–31 victory in 2018 over the Vikings.

59. B—9

60. Frank Filchock, Washington Redskins (October 8 and 15, 1939); Otto Graham, Cleveland Browns (September 12 and November 2, 1947); Peyton Manning, Indianapolis Colts (September 29, 2003, and January 1, 2004*); Ben Roethlisberger, Pittsburgh Steelers (November 5 and December 20, 2007); and Lamar Jackson, Baltimore Ravens (September 8 and November 10, 2019). *Game went to overtime.

Acknowledgments

This is my seventh book, and I can tell you unequivocally that the best part of the process—other than saying the words, "The manuscript is finished" out loud—is the acknowledgments. Thanking everyone who made it all possible. Writing is a strictly solitary pursuit, but the work of a book is a collaborative effort where the writer partners with multiple parties to reach the finish line. This one is no different.

Superagent Alec Shane remains without peer. There's no one else I'd rather ride into battle with. (And here's to another lunch at Keens sooner rather than later.) In addition, Jason Katzman at Sports Publishing was dynamite to work with throughout the process. (Maybe the first documented case of a Patriots fan and Giants fan working together for a common good?)

Big thanks to my colleagues, particularly Nicole Yang and Ben Volin of the *Boston Globe*, as well as my *Bleav* podcast partners Chris Hogan and LeGarrette Blount. I am smarter for having the honor of being in your company on a regular basis.

Pro Football Reference remains the gold standard of football statistical sites. Their site is indispensable to me in my daily work—and it made the verification process for a project like this one that much easier. All their reference sites are top notch. Go and visit them.

You don't write a book on your own; you need a lot of scaffolding in place. Our community of neighbors and friends help keep it all together, from the Northeastern crew and their significant others to people who have become so vital to our Metrowest experience. You're all world-class.

But at the heart of everything remains family: Dad, Kelly, Jas, Molly, Marc, Mina, and Trevor. My guy Justin Franklin—the biggest Shadeur Sanders fan out there—helped provide inspiration for this project. And finally, I'm blessed with the best home-field advantage any sportswriter could ever hope to have: Kate and Noah, and our cats, Boots and Scout. Team Price remains undefeated.

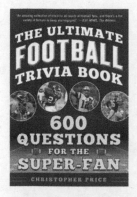